Branding & Graphic Design
Packaging Design
New Media Design
Interior, Retail & Event Design

BRITISH DESIGN 2010

BIS Publishers bv
Het Sieraad Building
Postjesweg 1
1057 DT Amsterdam
The Netherlands

T +31 (0)20 515 02 30
F +31 (0)20 515 02 39
E bis@bispublishers.nl
www.bispublishers.nl

© 2009 BIS Publishers, Amsterdam

ISBN 978 90 6369 202 5

Branding & Graphic Design
Packaging Design
New Media Design
Interior, Retail & Event Design

BRITISH DESIGN 2010

CONTENTS

DRINK'S PRICE LIST

HOT DRINK'S	£
TEA	50
COFFEE	60
MILKY COFFEE	£1 00
HOT CHOCOLATE	80
CUP·A SOUP	80
HOT BOVRIL	60

COLD DRINK S	£
CAN'S	60
BOTTLE S	
MILK	
WATER	60

BACON SAU?
PIE & CHIP
PASTY CHIP
1/2 LB BURGER
1/4 LB CHEESE
HAM EGG
~~MUSHROOM~~
1/4 LB BURGE
1/4 LB CHEESE

DESIGN AGENCIES BY LOCATION

FOREWORD

Welcome to *British Design 2010*, the fourth edition of BIS Publishers' cross-section of design studios and creative consultancies in Britain. We are proud to offer the British creative industry and its domestic and international clients this completely new, fourth survey of creative talent from the UK. The changes in the design industry over the last two years are of course reflected in this book and we are proud to say that more than ever before new creative studios have found their way to its pages, along with many established firms that are in here again because they have experienced the benefits of getting their work out to the national and international audience of design buyers who use the book.

The goal of this book is simple: to help clients in their search for the ideal design partner. *British Design 2010* provides an instant impression of each participating agency's work – it is a reference tool for whenever professional creative input is needed.

In his introductory article, design writer Ben Terret sketches a gloomy picture of the British design industry in recession. Which is in some cases good for clients, because also good things spring out of adversity. The question is, will it be business as usual when the economic wind takes another shift, or will designers and clients work together and see the special circumstances as an opportunity to really improve things and better use each other's expertise? As Ben Terret says, 'We live in a world we can control less than at any other point in history, but a world that needs designers more than ever.'

So talk more to designers – and why not to one of the fine studios in this book?

Rudolf van Wezel
BIS Publishers

BRITISH DESIGN 2010

BY BEN TERRETT

There is no witty intro to this piece.

The biggest issue affecting design in Britain is the recession. And it doesn't seem right to wrap that up in jokes and clever word play.

It's the first major economic downturn of my working life. It's very real and it's scary. Friends of mine have been made redundant. Clients have been made redundant. Big, well-known agencies have been cutting staff. Big, well-known agencies have gone bust. Clients have been cutting fees. Clients have gone bust. A friend of mine was made redundant whilst abroad – on business.

On my blog, I ran a series of guest posts from people who'd been through several recessions. Almost all of the advice was applicable to the good times too – it's just more important in a recession. Basic business skills become essential to staying alive. Watch your cash flow like a hawk, don't start working without a PO number, don't work for cheap rates or for nothing. Understand where your costs are; some accountants say 85% of costs are fixed and only 15% are variable.

Obviously, in a recession new business strategies become increasingly desperate. On the johnson banks 'Thought for the week' blog, they posted tales of ridiculous approaches from agencies:

"CALLER: 'Hi, (client name here) you may recall we spoke [3; 6; 9; 12] months ago at [the DBA/D&AD/Benchmarks/DW Awards; that conference you can't remember attending; Sainsbury's] just thought I'd drop you a line to see how you're getting on' ME: 'Oh, hi, yeah how are you? (secretly thinking how did they get through our dragons on reception?) CALLER: 'That's great' (clearly not listening) 'Well I just wanted to say that we've been really busy here doing some fantastic work on [insert unrelated client work] and would really like to come and present to you'

They also listed some types of approaches clients hated:

When they send you something stupid and expensive through the post, like a lollipop, or a slinky, or a mousetrap. These go in the recycling bin unread, because sending people stupid expensive things is a sure sign of Zero Creativity.

But, as ever, there are interesting new things springing out of adversity. Cutting costs doesn't always have to mean cutting people, for example. Honda have won lots of praise for stopping their production line for four months, thus sparing the workers from compulsory redundancies. Staff received full basic pay for the first two months and around 60% thereafter; meanwhile the plant was completely refurbished while it was empty. That's smart.

"When they send you something stupid and expensive through the post, like a lollipop, or a slinky, or a mousetrap. These go in the recycling bin unread, because sending people stupid expensive things is a sure sign of Zero Creativity."

Closer to home, staff at advertising agency BBH have taken a 3.5% voluntary pay cut in the shape of a day's unpaid leave every month. Of course, your income is reduced but some people are seeing that as 12 extra days off a year. As Google have found out, giving staff extra time to pursue their interests can reap huge rewards.

One of the industries that boom in a recession is cliché generation. Old ones get wheeled out and new ones get invented. Look, here comes one now: lots of innovation happens during a downturn.

As Nigel Coates, professor of architecture at the Royal College of Art, said in a recent Guardian article, 'I've also been saying that recession isn't altogether a bad thing. Of course, I don't want people to lose their jobs, but there's been a lot of boring and plain bad new building during the boom years – frumpitecture, I call it. Young architects are unlikely to find an interesting job, or any job, in the coming months, so it's a good time for them to study, think and dream of what a next generation of architecture might be.'

We've had recessions before but what might be different this time is that we have a whole generation of people who are used to making new stuff happen fast. One of the reasons there has been so much innovation on the web is that the barriers to entry are so low. Have an idea, go home, bash out the code and launch to the world. There's a bit more to it than that, obviously, but we are living in a world where people are used to prototyping quickly and cheaply.

Here's another cliché: recessions are a good time to prototype. Decisions can often be made quicker. New ideas don't get bogged down in process. People take risks because they have to. Better to fail quickly and cheaply rather than pay a management consultancy £1M to work out

"We've had recessions before but what might be different this time is that we have a whole generation of people who are used to making new stuff happen fast"

whether it will work. The new way to make ideas happen is to prototype instead of to PowerPoint. These days, people are also used to launching ideas before they're finished. Sharing work in progress and using the community to build upon it. Take Dave Gray's Marks and Meaning book. Gray realised that online publishing service Lulu have made the mechanics of book-making very cheap and easy. The best way to write a book is gather all your notes and rough thoughts together and stick them in a book. Then you can ask others to build on that until you're ready to print another version. It's a prototype book.

In addition to all this, we're entering a Post Digital age. People are becoming less impressed by screens. We're living in a time where stuff is migrating from the screen into the real world of objects. Possibilities in community, conversation, collaboration and creativity are turning out real things, real events, real places, real objects. The Web of Things, people have been calling this. A world where Print On Demand is becoming more accessible, where sites like Shapeways allow you to upload and then make 3D models quickly and cheaply. A world where 3D printers are getting cheaper and have just passed the point (£10,000) where desktop printers started to take off.

This is the other big issue facing design today. It's also very real and scary – less scary, but scary all the same. What does all this mean? What's it going to be like being a designer in this new world of austerity and the Internet of things? What will the client / designer relationship look like in 2011?

Tom Armitage and Matt Jones (both from London design consultancy Schulze & Webb) have talked about two new ideas I feel start to define this new world, a world where funding is hard to come by or comes attached with too many strings. Tom talks about Fanufacture. This is where you get fans to pay a premium to manufacture things that otherwise couldn't be produced. Maybe a handful of people would be willing to pay low four figures to make a few of something that would need millions of pounds to make the unit price low double figures.

Matt talks about the Thingfastructure. How we need to design media, services and products that are resilient, and self-sustaining as far as possible. We need to think about things from the start to the end, all the bits need to be able to communicate with each other, to scale up and down. Good examples of this are hard to find, but services like StreetCar and Howies' Hand Me Down range are close.

We're in the middle of a period where we're questioning basic economic models, so maybe this is a good time to question the business models of our industry. If you were starting a new company now, would you start a company? How would a major car brand have to change when the need to own a car is replaced by the need to have access to a car whenever you need one? How does a fashion brand feel when it sells products that last for decades, not seasons? How can you design things that are designed to be remixed and remade? We've got to think about all this as well as watching cash flow like a hawk and not working without a PO number.

These things affect all of us. Whether you're a packaging designer or a product designer. Whether you're a brand guru or you write a blog you print through Lulu. The recession and the Web of Things are colliding to create a scary yet fertile environment. It's up to us to determine whether we turn that into an opportunity or just another spin of the economic wheel.

We live in a world we can control less than at any other point in history, but a world that needs designers more than ever.

Ben Terrett is a designer and a partner in Really Interesting Group www.reallyinterestinggroup.com/

He's also a Board Advisor to id8 based in San Francisco, and prior to that, he founded The Design Conspiracy. This is his first recession.

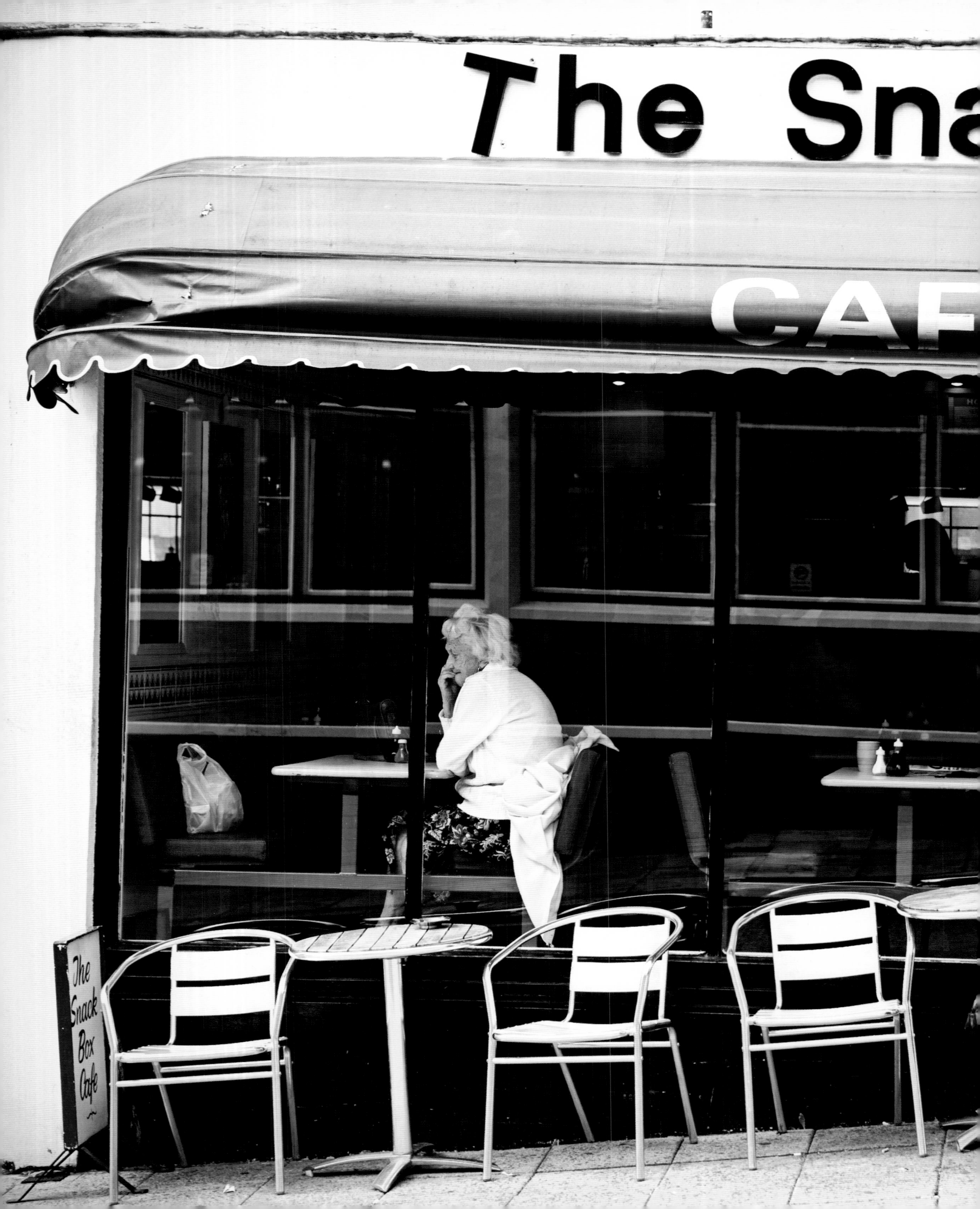
The Sna
CAF
The Snack Box Cafe

BRANDING
& GRAPHIC
DESIGN

Accept & Proceed
Design & Art Direction

Studio 2 / Peachy Edwards House /
1 Teesdale Street / London E2 6GF
T +44 (0)20 7199 1030
info@acceptandproceed.com
www.acceptandproceed.com

Management David Johnston, Managing Director
Matthew Jones, Creative Director
Staff 5 **Founded** 2006

Company Profile
Established in 2006, Accept & Proceed is a Design
and Art Direction facility working in a wide range of
sectors including the Music, Fashion and Advertising
Industries. Based in the East End of London, we are
a close-knit team of creatives that create innovative,
concept-driven work. Our current clients include
Nike, Wrangler, Google, Manhattan Loft Corporation,
Christian Aid and Sony. Creative experimentation
is at the core of what we do, as is the continual
development of non-commercial projects, both
personal and in collaboration. Internationally
experienced, we have won several Art Direction
awards for our clients.

1 Now in its third year, the Loop Digital Culture
   Festival is Brighton's annual Summer music
   event for over 5,000 revellers. Accept & Proceed
   have created all visual output for the event since
   the beginning.
   Following on from the success of last years
   campaign (which was featured on the cover of
   Creative Review's Photography Annual) this year
   we have created a physical representation of
   the loop logo, interpreted as sound. By starting
   with an image, turning it into sound, and then
   documenting again as an image, we have
   created a loop.

   David Ellis shot the intriguing installation, which
   was created over two days at Studio 19 in
   Dalston.

2-6 A series of five graphs produced in 2008 for K2,
   a business performance management company
   which looks at systems and approaches
   employed by some of the worlds elite athletes,
   and applies them to a business context.

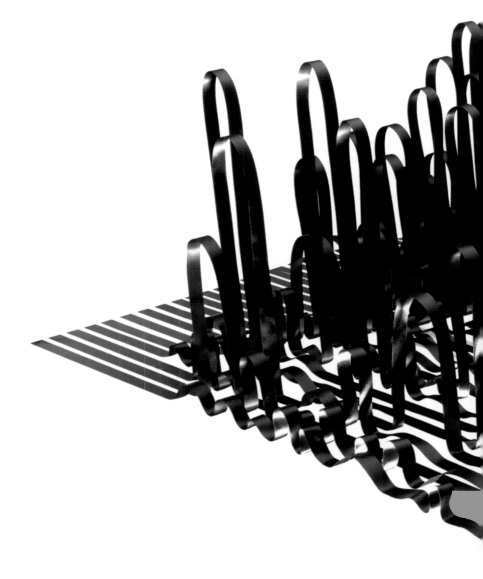

1

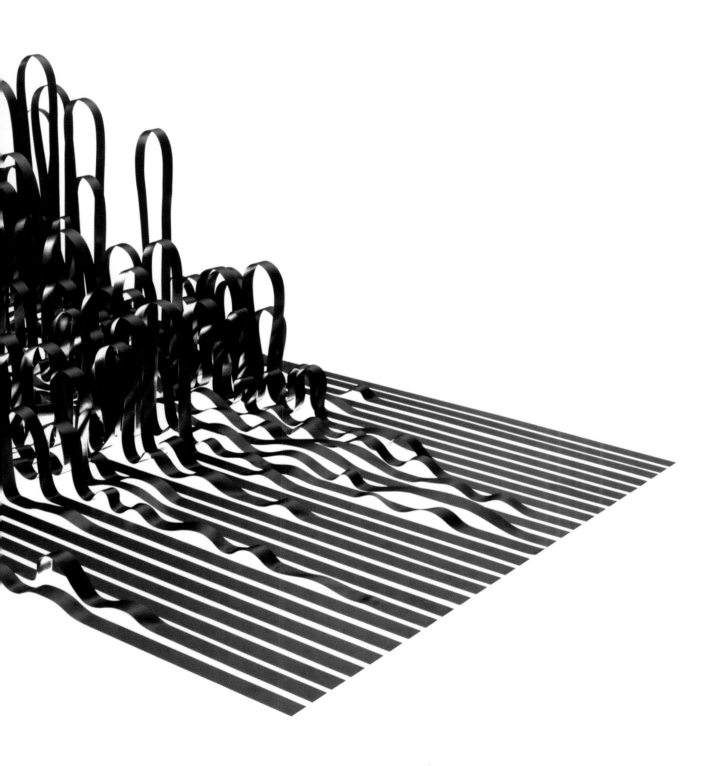

Tiger Woods vs. Rocco Mediate

12th – 15th June 2008
U.S. Open Golf Championships
Torrey Pines, San Diego, California.

	01 Tiger Rocco	02 Tiger Rocco	03 Tiger Rocco	04 Tiger Rocco	05 Tiger Rocco	06 Tiger Rocco	07 Tiger Rocco	08 Tiger Rocco	09 Tiger Rocco	10 Tiger Rocco	11 Tiger Rocco	12 Tiger Rocco	13 Tiger Rocco	14 Tiger Rocco	15 Tiger Rocco	16 Tiger Rocco	17 Tiger Rocco	18 Tiger Rocco	Score Tiger Rocco
Round 1	6 4	4 4	3 2	3 3	4 4	4 4	4 5	2 3	4 5	4 4	3 3	4 4	5 4	6 5	4 4	3 3	4 4	5 4	72 69
Round 2	3 4	3 3	3 3	3 3	3 4	4 4	4 4	3 3	4 5	5 5	3 3	5 5	3 5	4 4	4 4	4 3	5 5	5 4	68 71
Round 3	6 4	4 4	3 2	5 3	4 4	4 4	3 5	3 3	5 5	4 4	3 3	5 4	3 4	5 5	4 4	3 3	3 4	3 4	70 72
Round 4	6 4	5 3	3 3	4 4	4 5	4 5	4 4	3 3	4 5	4 3	2 3	4 4	6 5	4 3	5 5	3 3	4 4	4 5	73 71
18 Hole Playoff	4 5	4 4	4 2	4 4	4 5	3 4	3 4	4 3	5 6	4 5	4 3	5 4	4 4	4 3	4 3	3 3	4 4	4 5	71 71
Sudden Death Playoff	4 5																		4 5

Accept & Proceed
Elite Sporting Moment Series 3 of 5

3

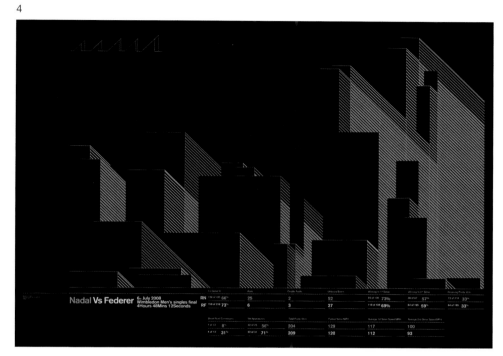

4

Nadal **Vs** Federer

5

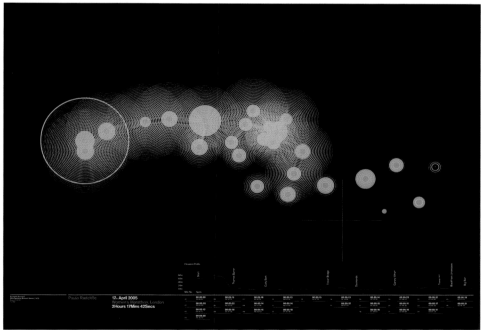

6

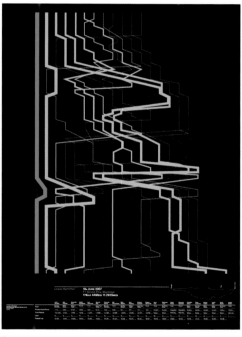

Bark Design Limited

Studio 5 / Panther House 38 / Mount Pleasant /
London WC1X 0AP
T +44 (0)207 8373116 / F +44 (0)207 8373116
bark@barkdesign.net
www.barkdesign.net

Contacts Tim Hutchinson, Jason Edwards
Founded 1995

Company Profile
Bark was established by fellow Royal College of
Art graduates, Tim Hutchinson and Jason Edwards
in 1995. They head up a team of people that have
created design briefs for clients as diverse as Rankin,
Sony, Nigel Coates and Deutsche Bank.

Bark has been committed to delivering the best
bespoke solutions in line with the needs of the clients.
Their understanding of contemporary culture makes
them competent in the consultancy and design of
branding including identity, publication, promotion
and packaging in print and online.

"Bark, are a boutique agency who can deliver and
execute big ideas, with passion and unbaffling
rationale"
Sony PlayStation UK

"Knowledge of client business practices allow Bark to
support our need to drive revenue through insightful
and customer targetted design"
Andaz Liverpool Street / London

Clients
Sony PlayStation
Deutsche Bank
John Doe
Andaz, Liverpool Street
Proud Galleries
Metropolitan Film School
Teenage Cancer Trust
Summers Trust
Shine Communications
ZincOx Plc
MADE

1 Identity design, brand creation & application for
   '1901', the flagship restaurant for Andaz Liverpool
   Street hotel, London.
2 Art direction, Design and photography for
   www.andazdining.com, a website that provides
   an online platform for all five restaurants at
   Andaz Liverpool Street plus other dining facilities
   at the hotel. The website acts as an online
   brochure experience for each restaurant plus
   booking options.
3 Identity design and application, print and screen
   based for John Doe PR.

JOHN DOE

1 Hardwick Street
London
EC1R 4RB

T: 020 7841 7091
F: 020 7100 7171

Email
info:none@johndoehub.com
www.johndoehub.com

The Brand Union
The Global Brand Agency

11-33 St John Street / London EC1M 4AA
T +44 (0)20 7559 7000 / F +44 (0)20 7559 7001
info@thebrandunion.com
www.thebrandunion.com

Contacts Simon Bailey, UK CEO
Terry Tyrrell, Worldwide Chairman

Company Profile
The Brand Union is a world-class global brand
agency, comprising 500 people across 21 offices.
What binds us together is a deep-seated commitment
to becoming masters of the art and science of brand
building. In all our disciplines, Brand Mastery is our
central organising thought.

We help brands grow. We offer direction. We protect
brands against the economic and cultural elements.
Bright ideas guide us – they are the lifeblood of our
business. And we take pride in crafting and shaping
the brightest ideas into memorable and valuable
brand worlds.

We have created identities for some of the world's
leading brands including American Express, Absolut
and Bank of America.

We have delivered product branding and brand
environments for clients such as SABMiller,
Masterfoods, Unilever, Motorola and Diageo.

And we have helped grow and position corporate
giants like Canon, Credit Suisse, Corus, Deloitte and
Vodafone.

Our services include Research, Strategy, Design,
Engagement and Evaluation.

At The Brand Union, we believe that brands are an
organisation's most important asset. We admire
companies that see everything they do as brand –
that understand the power of brand-driven growth.
We help corporate brands stay relevant to their
customer base all over the world and we help turn
brand challenges into brand opportunities. Whether
it's reinvigorating your corporate identity, reinforcing
your brand values, or developing consistency across
a global brand platform, we have the skill and the
experience to guide companies in building memorable
and enduring brand worlds.

Clients
Alfa Romeo
Bacardi
Barclaycard
Canon
Deutsche Post
HSBC
Reckitt Benckiser
SABMiller
Swedish Post
Vodafone

**See also Packaging Design p.120 and New Media
Design p.162**

Build

Studio 112 / Hilton Grove / 12–15 Hatherley Mews /
London E17 4QP
T +44 (0)208 5211040
informyou@wearebuild.com
www.wearebuild.com

Management Michael & Nicola Place
Contact Nicola Place
Staff 3 **Founded** 2001

Company Profile

Build is a Graphic Design studio based in London,
UK. Established in 2001 by Creative Director Michael
C. Place, Build has since forged an international
reputation as a forward-thinking studio, with an
exceptional eye for detail and a unique sense of style.
The studio is run by Michael C. Place and Nicola
Place and is well-known for its passion for print, type
and the craft of design. The studio produces a wide
range of graphic work from illustration, brand identity,
design & layout as well as art direction for print,
websites and animation.

Build has shown its works in several exhibitions in
the UK & abroad, most recently producing exclusive
print artworks for display within The North Face
stores in Japan.

Michael features in the 2007 film 'Helvetica —
A Documetary Film', has spoken at numerous
conferences worldwide, & has twice been a judge
at the prestigious D&AD global awards.

Clients

Our client list includes Getty Images, Nike,
Design Museum London, D&AD, Sony Computer
Entertainment and Faber&Faber publishing, amongst
a host of smaller independents.

1 Not For Commercial Use – Postcard pack
2 Not For Commercial Use – Postcard pack (open)
3 Not For Commercial Use – Poster: Manifesto
4 Not For Commercial Use – Poster: Test-card 1
5 Not For Commercial Use – Poster:
   Dendrochronology
6 Not For Commercial Use – Poster: Symbiosis
7 Not For Commercial Use – Poster: Statement
8 Not For Commercial Use – Catalogue

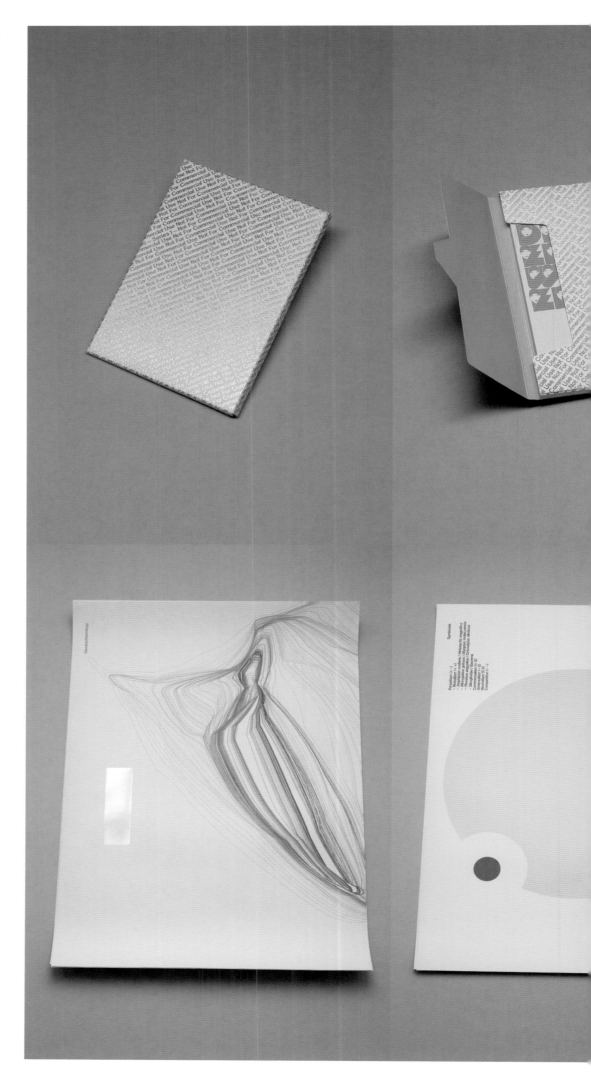

Not For Commercial Use
Not For Sale
Not For Resale
Not For Profit
Not For Re-Release
Not For Distribution
Flickr tags — Not, Non,
"Non-Commercial"
Do Not eBay This Poster
Take Down Carefully And
Display At Home
For You,
For Everyone.

ALL
DESIGN-
ERS ARE
WANK-
ERS.

Not For Commercial Use
An idea by
&
ISBN 0 9545609 5 1
First published by
Generation Yacht 2007
generationyacht.com

24 page document

CampbellRigg

8 Apollo Studios / Charlton Kings Road /
London NW5 2SB
T +44 (0)20 7284 1515
F +44 (0)20 7267 4112
design@campbellrigg.com
www.campbellrigg.com

Management Campbell Rigg, Dorota Czernuszewicz
Contact Dorota Czernuszewicz
Founded 1987

Company Profile
CampbellRigg has over 20 years of experience
providing strategic and creative design solutions
for some of the world's most successful companies.

An independent agency, we are renowned
for our international work in retail interiors and
communications across a broad range of markets
including food and non-food, textiles and banking.
The quality of our work has been recognised with
National and International awards from industry-
leading publications such as Retail Week and
Retail Interiors.

We believe in retail design excellence – using
imagination, intuition and financial common sense
to find the right solution. We can add real economic
value to your retail business using our extensive
experience in providing the following services:

- Strategy
- Brand Creation & Corporate Identity
- Graphic Communication
- Retail Interiors & Architecture
- Format Planning
- Merchandising
- Project Implementation

Our skilled multilingual team of strategic planners,
interior & graphic designers and architects have
worked with clients based across the globe including:

Austria: Interspar AG
Finland: Kesko OY
Germany: Adler GmbH (Metro), Kaufhof AG (Metro),
OBI GmbH (Tengelmann)
Ireland: Musgrave
Russia: Investproject, Victoria
Sweden: ICA OY, Hennes & Mauritz OY
Switzerland: Manor AG, Ukraine, Continium

United Kingdom: Asda (Wal-Mart), Argos, Arcadia,
Bacardi Global Retail, Blockbuster (UK) Ltd, Courtald
Textiles plc, Country Casuals, Comet Group plc,
Dixon Stores plc, Interbrew (UK) Ltd, Harrods
Ltd, Harvey Nichols plc, Marks and Spencer plc,
McDonalds Ltd, Safeway plc, Tesco plc, Unilever plc

Recent Awards
Retail Week 2009 Store Design of the Year (Finalist)
Retail Interiors 2006 Best In-Store
Communications (Winner)

See also Interior, Retail and Event Design p. 188

bellrigg

brand design excellence

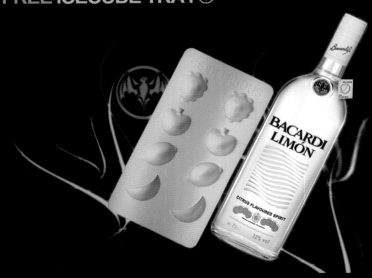

GETDELICIOUS
FREE ICECUBE TRAY

Bacardi Global Travel Retail

Chaos

Head Office:
32 High Street / Guildford / Surrey GU1 3EL
Offices: Guildford, London and Lausanne
T +44 (0)1483 557800 / F +44 (0)1483 537755
peter.c@chaosdesign.com
www.chaosdesign.com

Contact Peter Campbell, MD,
Creative and Brand Strategy
Staff 20 **Founded** 2002

Company Profile
Why Chaos?
Chaos Design Limited is an established independent
brand development and marketing communications
creative agency. We think strategically and also
act tactically. We provide inspiration and deliver
implementation through the line, offline and online.

Our creativity (Chaos Thinking™) helps enable a
brand to build awareness, heighten perception, attract
interest, increase sales and communicate effectively
with both external & internal audiences, shareholders
and investors. Chaos delivers Creative Enablement™

As an established agency we have built up a wealth
of client experience from a number of different market
sectors across b2b and b2c and we enjoy a number
of long term relationships with clients.

Chaos Design Limited is a leading creative agency,
ranked as a UK top 40 Design Agency.

Brand Development:
– Brand Identity
– Brand Management
– Brand Communications
– Creative Strategy

Marketing Communications:
– Literature
– Web / Digital eMedia
– Advertising/ Direct Mail
– Packaging / POS

Clients
Canon, Sony, BAA, BlackBerry, Dell, Bombardier
Osram, Christie+Co, Esporta, ESPA, Altria...
A full client history and list available upon request.

Awards
We know that... great clients & good briefs enable
brilliant ideas which deliver excellent results.
Our work has received awards for Marketing and
Design for both ourselves and our clients.

1 Brand development and marketing
  communications. Cyprus's largest 5 star leisure
  destination development.
2 Channel marketing campaign for new low energy
  efficient bulbs enabling greater brand awareness
  and market share.
3 Rebranding UK office supplies business (LGC).
  Brand name generation, brand management and
  creative brand strategy.
4 Launching a new hand santiser. Brand name
  generation, packaging design, integrated brand
  activation.
5 Online banner campaign part of an integrated
  marketing campaign.
6 Brand guidelines to launch a new brand
  strategy across EMEA. Brand development, brand
  management, guardianship and brand activation
  internally and externally through campaign
  implementation.

CONVENIENT

OUTSTANDING

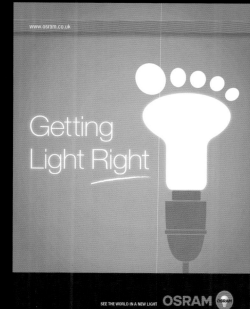

Getting
Light Right

SEE THE WORLD IN A NEW LIGHT   OSRAM

2

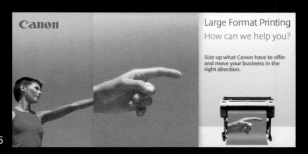

5

6

™

S

Crumpled Dog
Graphic Design

18 Phipp Street / London EC2A 4NU
T +44 (0)20 7739 5553
christian@crumpled-dog.com
www.crumpled-dog.com

Contacts Christian Stanley, Scott Leaver,
Adam Bass, Jeavon Leopold
Staff 9

Company Profile
Crumpled Dog is the leading identity design firm for
the professional services sector. We help companies
to deliver consistent, high-powered communications
in a wide range of mediums, giving them the power
to punch above their weight.

Expertise
Brand & Identity
Web
Creative Copywriting
Print
Exhibition

Business to business clients
Atom42
BEAMA
Buckley Gray Yeoman Architects
Churston Heard/Jones Lang LaSalle
Double Helix Research
Envestors
Lucent Lighting
MA Cherrington
National Grid
Oxford University Press
Red Loft
Smiths Group plc
The Research Partnership

Consumer clients
Ground Restaurants
East15 Acting School - Essex University
Euphorium Bakery
Gandini Juggling
Institute of Registered Valuers
National Accident Helpline
Sunstone Women
TrustMark
Zizzi Restaurants

Key Projects in 2008-2009
Euphorium Bakery - relaunch
National Grid on-line photography competition
Atom42 - identity and website
MA Cherrington website
Buckley Gray Yeoman website

A NATURAL PRODUCT MADE WITH LOVE FOR EUPHORIUM BAKERY

euphoriumbakery

heavenly honey

Euphorium Group Ltd, 202 Upper St. Islington N1 1RQ

euphorium bakery
the best of British baking

"you can never get a cup of tea large enough or a book long enough to suit me"
C S Lewis

"only dull people are brilliant at breakfast"
Oscar Wilde

...that make the difference between good and great baking. Without love and... affection ou...

bread, Walrus said
Lewis Ca...

euphorium baker...

"taste our sumptuous cakes and sample the best of British baking"
euphoriumbakery

euphoriumbakery
the best of British baking

euphoriumbakery

Join the British baking revolution!
(and claim your FREE coffee*)

NOW OPEN NOW...

Visit our newly opened bakery to sample succulent breads and seductive breads, pastries and cakes.

euphorium breads

It's not magic, ...nocellular organism...

CURIOUS

19a Floral Street / London WC2E 9DS
T +44 (0)20 7240 6214
claire@curiouslondon.com
www.curiouslondon.com

Contact Claire Syrett

Why are vultures bald?
What's the longest word in English?
Who invented the flushing toilet?
How do you make an egg nog?
That's the trouble with being curious. You start with
a perfectly reasonable quest for knowledge, and next
thing you want to know the answer to everything.

We started innocently enough. We were curious
about our clients' business. We were curious to know
things like: What's your brand all about? Who buys
whatever it is you sell? And why? What's your brand
communicating?

The great thing about asking interesting questions is,
you get interesting answers:
'Floccinaucinihilipilification', 'Thomas Crapper', and
'With difficulty', for example. And why are vultures
bald? Don't ask.

Design Disciplines
Branding
Corporate Identity
Digital
Advertising
Direct Mail
Print

Clients
Areen Design Services
Aviva
Barclays
Berwin Leighton Paisner
Clarion Retail
Close Brothers
Design Council
Electrolux
Film It
Hot Sauce Production
Norwich Union
Pighog Press
Richmond International
Sappi Fine Paper Europe
The South
Trolex
Virgin Money

Norwich Union

The Independent on Sunday

RAC

Knifey Spoony

Sappi Fine Paper Europe

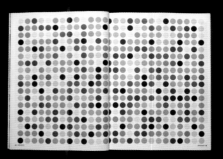

D.Vision Create

48 Fitzroy Street / London W1T 5BS
T +44 (0)20 7681 0001
contact@dvisioncreate.com
www.dvisioncreate.com

Contact Jonathan Davis
Founded 2002

Company Profile
D.Vision Create are an enthusiastic, focussed and intelligent marketing led design agency.

What we do is who we are... Working with a wide variety of premium brands from sectors as diverse as finance, beauty, product, property and retail, D.Vision Create are a team of highly experienced creatives and strategic thinkers passionate about producing stunning and applicable design. We strive to excel in creativity and innovation while still being effective in answering both the client brief and more importantly, in its engagement with their target audiences. A dedicated and responsive team ensures everyone who works with us gets 100%+ attention, regardless of the size or scope of the project.
We will support your marketing needs in every way we can, ensuring that you get the results you need.

Our Services
Branding
Graphic Communications
Digital Media
Strategy & Planning
Fun!

Molton Brown   New West End Company   Palmerston Resort Etna

IG Index   Renault Formula 1 Team Collection   MF Global   Humanscale

Design Project

Second Floor / 80A York Street / Leeds LS9 8AA
T +44 (0)113 234 1222
james@designproject.co.uk
www.designproject.co.uk

Management James Littlewood, Andy Probert
Contact James Littlewood
Founded 2004

Company Profile
Design Project have a history of creating distinctive visual communications that deliver outstanding results for clients in industry, the service sector, media and the arts.

Across brand identity, print and digital media, our multi-disciplinary approach ensures that every project, regardless of scale or budget, results in a functional, effective and crafted solution that fulfils the communication objectives of the client.

Clients
ArjoWiggins Fine Papers
Burmatex
Corporate Workspace
Creative Review
D&AD
DLG Architects
Fedrigoni UK
Henry Moore Foundation
Leeds Art Gallery
Manchester International Festival
Oblong Furniture
P+HS Architects
Progress Packaging
Robert Horne Group
Senator International
SLS Solicitors
St James Securities
Tate Liverpool
Team Impression
Yorkshire Sculpture Park

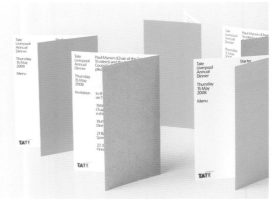

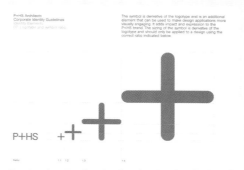
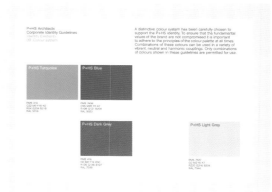

P+HS

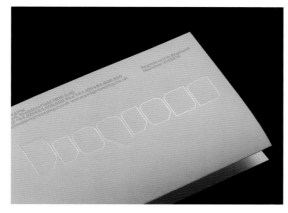

Designhouse
Design Consultants

T +44 (0)20 8439 9360 / F +44 (0)20 8439 9373
74 Great Suffolk Street / London SE1 0BL
dh@designhouse.co.uk
www.designhouse.co.uk

Management Lavinia Culverhouse
Contact Lavinia Culverhouse
Founded 1970

Company Profile
We invent, revitalise, express, expand and discover the brilliance in brands.

We focus upon achieving better commercial returns for our clients.

These two thoughts drive us – just as they have done since we began in 1970.

Our solutions deliver results, winning 9 International Design Business Association Awards and receiving 20 nominations.

Clients
BT
BUPA
B&Q
Career Moves Group
City Inn
Dufry
Ebel
ING
John Lewis
Ladbrokes
Land Securities
NHS
Royal Bank of Scotland
Royal Mail

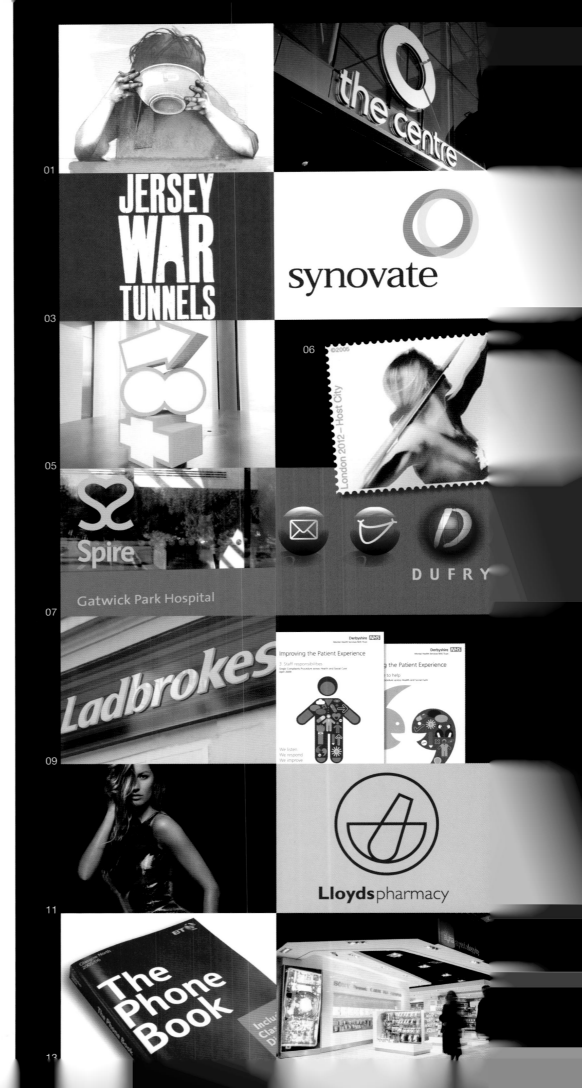

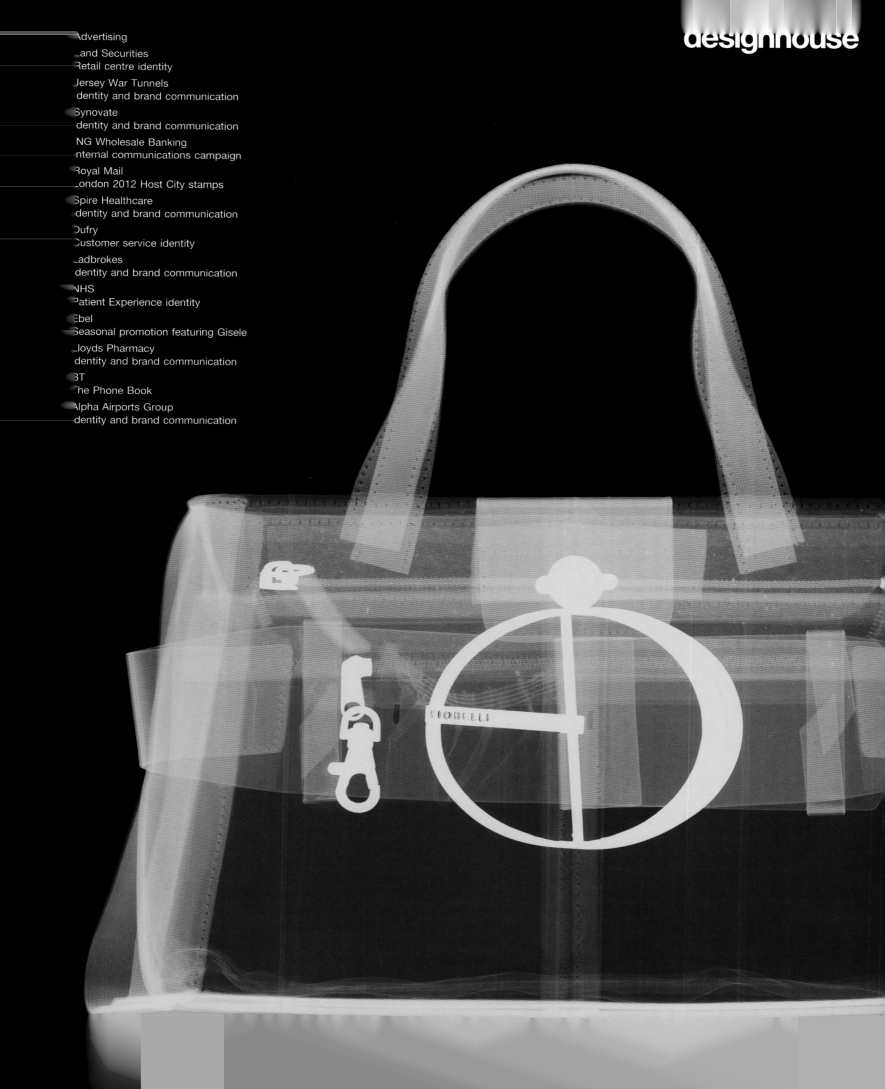

designhouse

Element 5.0
Design & Communication

14 Blandford Square / Newcastle upon Tyne NE1 4HZ
T +44 (0)191 255 4420 / F +44 (0)191 255 4421
info@element5design.com
www.element5design.com

Management Trevor Bolam, Rob Jackson,
Ewan McCann, Tom McCarthy
Contact Rob Jackson
Staff 10 **Founded** 2000

Company Profile
Element 5.0 is a graphic design and communication
consultancy based in Newcastle upon Tyne.
Producing design of clarity, relevance and originality,
we strongly believe in the power of graphic
communication to make a difference — whether
to increase sales, position a brand, or simply to
get noticed. We care about what we do. We are
passionate about design and committed to
creative excellence.

Expertise
Brand Identity & Implementation
Corporate Communications
Consultancy
Digital Communications
Exhibitions
Graphic Design
Promotional Literature
Web Design

01

02

03

04

05

06

High Frequency Economics®
Daily Data Analysis and Assessment of the Global Economy

Join the revolution today at
www.children-of-the-revolution.co.uk

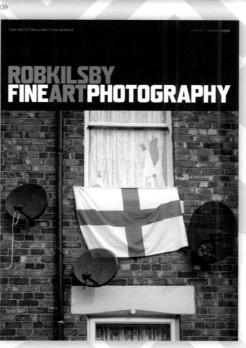

07

08

09

10

11

12

13

14

15

01 County Durham Sport. Brand Identity & Communications
02 Nexus. Poster Campaign
03 Zanders Hair Design. Brand Identity & Launch Campaign
04 Natural Warmth. Brand Identity
05 The Old Co-op Buildings. Branding & Promotional Brochure
06 Unpublished. 'Reclaiming Disco' A2 Poster
07 High Frequency Economics. Brand Identity & Communications
08 The Arrow. Branding & Promotional Posters
09 Children Of The Revolution. Brand Identity & Promotion
10 Rob Kilsby Photography. Branding & Limited Edition Posters
11 Mark Collett Design & Build. Brand Identity
12 Packed4U. Brand Identity & Launch Campaign
13 Lifestyle International. Brand Identity & Promotional Literature
14 Self-Promotion. Limited Edition Print
15 Komatsu 1in4. Brand Identity & Communications

Felton Communication

2 Bleeding Heart Yard / London EC1N 8SJ
T +44 (0)20 7405 0900 / F +44 (0)20 7430 1550
design@felton.co.uk
www.feltonworks.com

Management Roger Felton, Glenn Reynolds,
Katherine Felton
Contacts Roger Felton, Glenn Reynolds,
Juliette Mauve, Michael Skipper
Staff 12 **Founded** 1989

Company Profile
Over 20 years, we've won over 50 awards, retained
over 80% of our clients and delivered well over
10,000 thousand successful projects. From brand
identities and literature systems to campaigns and
websites, our work changes hearts and minds.

Our longevity is based on three ingredients:
understanding, commitment and creativity.

Understanding:
Whether we're working with chief executives, lawyers
or civil servants, our starting point remains the same:
the importance of understanding our client's business.

We research their issues. We ask questions of them.
We ask questions of their audiences. We diagnose
their uniqueness. And then we turn that thinking into
logically lateral creative ideas that work.

Commitment:
Whether we're working with charities, government
departments or multinational organisations, our
attitude remains the same: we're committed.

Our focus is on you. Our focus is on your needs. Our
focus is on your customers. And judging from our
client (and staff) retention rate, it's an approach that
seems to work.

Creativity:
Whether your customers are sexually active, socially
excluded or significantly valuable, our approach is
consistent: creativity that works.

Ideas that win hearts. Ideas that change minds. Ideas
that make a real difference.

Clients
BAA
Dental Defence Union
Family Mosaic
International AIDS Alliance
Lambeth Council
NHS
Pure Recruitment
Terrence Higgins Trust
TMA World
Transport for London
Trollope Society
Living Streets
Women's Sport and Fitness Foundation
v
Volume Developments

Awards
5 DBA Design Effectiveness Awards
3 CIB Communications Strategy Awards
4 British Medical Association Awards
4 PAMADA Property Marketing Awards
3 National Housing Federation Awards
UK Housing Award
Marketing Brand Design Award
London International Advertising Award
CIPFA Public Reporting Award
....and a Chip Shop Award

For effective corporate and campaign identities... and a nice cup of tea. **FELTON** works.com

FL@33
multi-disciplinary design studio for visual communication

59 Britton Street / London EC1M 5UU
T +44 (0)20 7168 7990
contact@flat33.com
flat33.com
stereohype.com
bzzzpeek.com
postcard-book.info
madeandsold.com

Management Agathe Jacquillat MA (RCA),
Tomi Vollauschek MA (RCA)
Staff 2 **Founded** 2001

Company Profile

FL@33 is a multi-disciplinary studio for visual communication based in London. Its founders, Agathe Jacquillat (French, from Paris) and Tomi Vollauschek (Austrian, but from Frankfurt, Germany), studied at FH Darmstadt (Germany), Academy Julian/ ESAG (Penninghen) (Paris), HDK (Gothenburg) and Camberwell College of Art (London), before they met on the Royal College of Art's postgraduate Communication Art and Design course in 1999.

They set up their company in London in 2001. The studio's clients include MTV Networks, BBC, Royal Festival Hall, Laurence King Publishing, Creative Review, Computer Arts, Groupe Galeries Lafayette, Matelsom, Arts Affaires and Friends of the Earth.

The two launched Stereohype.com – Graphic Art & Fashion Boutique – in 2004: an international platform for both emerging and established talents. The duo have also released self-initiated projects such as the award-winning Trans-form magazine and online sound collection project bzzzpeek.com.

FL@33 interviews, features and company profiles have been published online, in numerous magazines, newspapers and books around the world. Interviews featured on BBC Radio and NPR, America's National Public Radio, after The New York Times, along with its international supplements, featured an article about the bzzzpeek.com project.

A FL@33 monograph was published in 2005 as part of the bilingual (English and French) design&designer book series by French Pyramyd Editions.

In 2008 Laurence King published Postcard – a book FL@33 have conceived, compiled, written, edited and designed. Foreign language editions of Postcard were released by DuMont (German), Pyramyd (French) and Gustavo Gili (Spanish).

Made & Sold: Toys, T-Shirts, Prints, Zines and Other Stuff is the second book by FL@33 and was published by Laurence King in October 2009.

Selected FL@33 projects 2001–2009

FOUR IV

11 Northburgh Street / London EC1V 0AN
T +44 (0)20 7336 1344 / F +44 (0)20 7336 1345
simont@fouriv.com
www.fouriv.com

Management Chris Dewar Dixon, Andy Bone,
Simon Thompson
Contact Simon Thompson
Staff 28 **Founded** 1989

Company Profile
FOUR IV is a leading UK based graphic and interior
design agency.

Specialising in brand development and retail & leisure
interior design, FOUR IV is the creative agency behind
some of the world's most exciting and commercially
proven luxury retail and leisure brands.

Currently working in over 14 countries, we are now in
our 20th year.

Clients
Browns
Burberry
Emporio Armani
Dunhill
Dinny Hall
Duchamp
Gas
Gieves and Hawkes
Hawkshead
Kurt Geiger
Liberty
Luella
Mulberry
Thomas Pink
Timberland
American Golf
Boots
DFS
Habitat
Mamas and Papas
Sothebys
Wedgwood
Harvey Nichols
Harrods
John Lewis Partnership
Arnotts
Unitim
Fenwick
Bouwfonds MAB
CBRE
Westfield
Abu Dhabi Tourism Authority
Athenæum
The Grove
InterContinental
Jumeirah Beach
Runnymede
The Langham
Nyonya
First Choice
Carlton Savannah Hotel
Utell

**See also New Media Design p. 166 and Interior,
Retail and Event Design p. 194**

NAKED, ISTANBUL

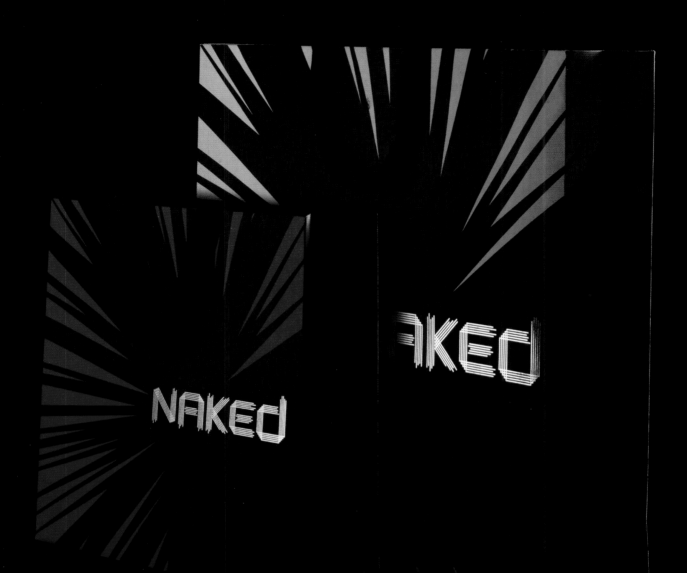

ABU DHABI TOURISM AUTHORITY

HARVEY NICHOLS

THE ATHENAEUM

DUCHAMP

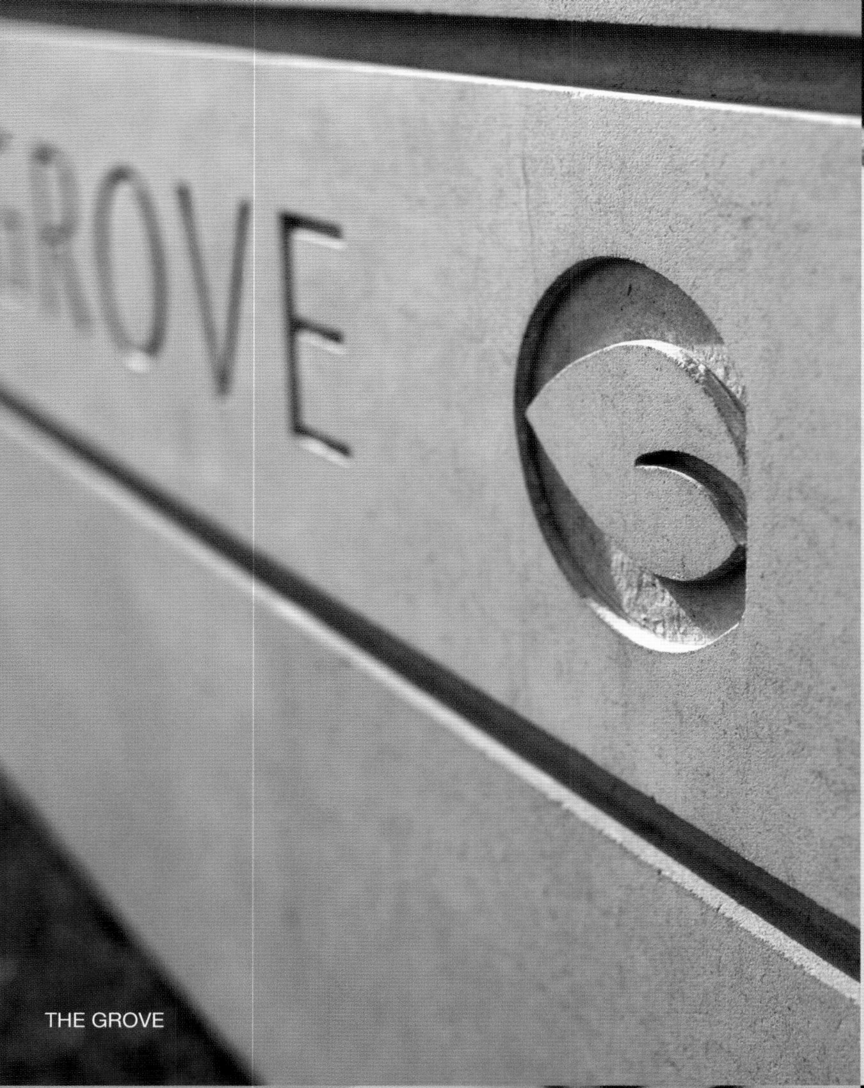

THE GROVE

PEMBROKE REAL ESTATE

GREAT PORTLAND ESTATES

THE LANGHAM

Gensler

Aldgate House / 33 Aldgate High Street /
London EC3N 1AH
T +44 (0)207 073 9600
duncan_mackay@gensler.com
www.gensler.com

Company Profile

Creating great brands is about unlocking the potential of a place, organisation or company to tell a powerful story, one built from its intrinsic characteristics and values. Like any story, a great brand begins with a meaningful idea that inspires design, drives an experience and engages people on an emotional level.

Our services range from brand strategy to user experience design, graphic design (identity, business systems and collateral), and environmental graphic design (placemaking, signage and wayfinding).

Clients

ADCB
Alghanim X-cite
Al Mazaya
Blackstone Group
Chevrolet
Haworth
McGregor
London Stock Exchange
MS Retail - Baroue
Paragon
Royal Bank of Scotland
Selfridges
Suit Supply
World Retail Congress

See also Interior, Retail and Event Design p. 198

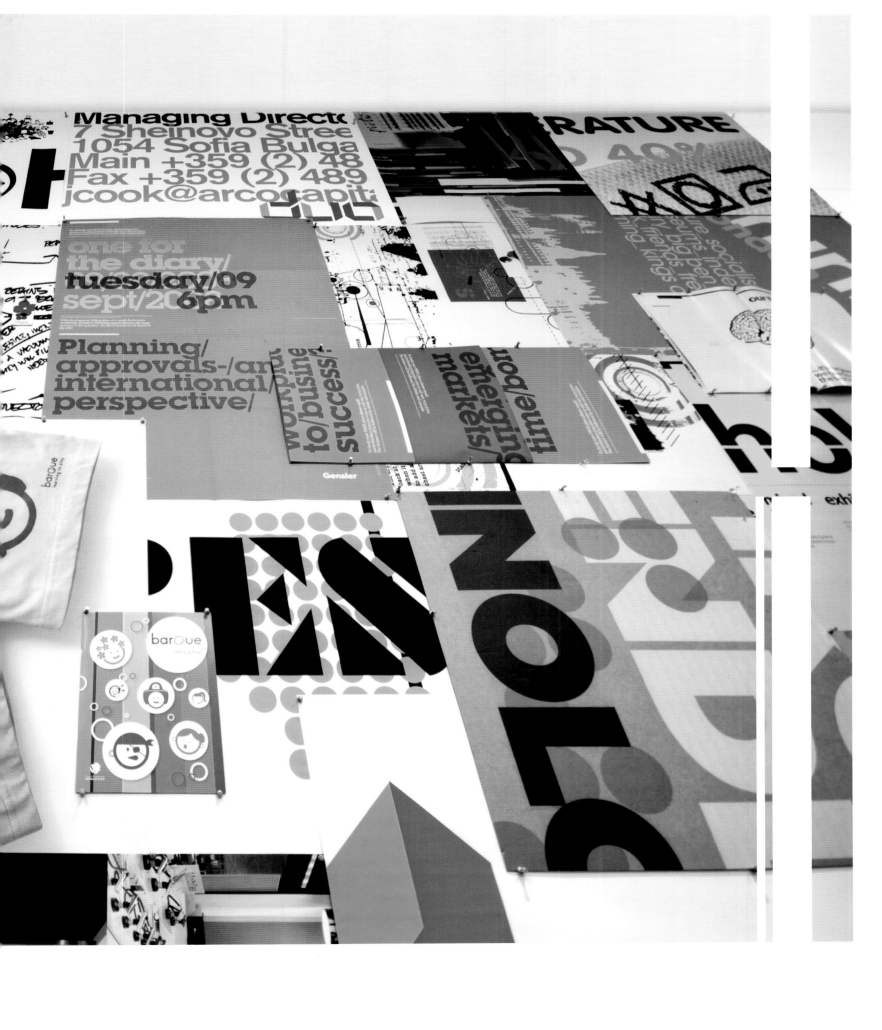

Greenwich Design

David Mews / 11a Greenwich South Street /
Greenwich / London SE10 8NJ
T +44 (0)20 8853 3028 / F +44 (0)20 8858 2128
hello@greenwich-design.co.uk
www.greenwich-design.co.uk

Management Simon Wright MD
Contacts Simon Wright, Mary Davidson
Staff 12 **Founded** 1966

Company Profile
For over forty (yes, forty) years, Greenwich Design
has been fusing images and words for a diverse client
base that includes both multinationals and start-up
businesses.

Cool analysis. Strategic evaluation. Creative brio. All
this and more we apply to graphic communications
across the board, including identity creation,
branding, packaging, literature, advertising and
multimedia.

Here's what our client at Greenwich PCT said
about us:

"They're the best looking NHS documents I've ever
seen! Your ability to interpret, amplify, create and then
deliver such wonderful products from an original idea
has me overwhelmed. Jubilation, pride, satisfaction –
it's a heady mix!"

Greenwich Design.
Where fluid thinking takes shape.

Clients
A1GP
Andrews Sykes
Brooke Bond Oxo
Cypressa
Dorling Kindersley
Ferrari
Greenwich PCT
Marks and Spencer
Marley Waterproofing
Pentel
Shell International
Trinity College of Music

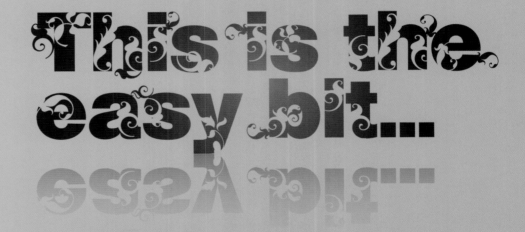

[INFORM]

...but our stylish, seductive graphics are built on a thorough
understanding of how brands work. We'll get to the warm
squishy heart of your proposition and deliver communications
that speak the right visual language.

Tom Hingston Studio
Design and Art Direction

76 Brewer Street / London W1F 9TX
T +44 (0)20 7287 6044 / F +44 (0)20 7287 6048
info@hingston.net
www.hingston.net

Staff 5 **Founded** 1997

Company Profile
Established in 1997, Tom Hingston Studio is an
independent multi-disciplinary design agency.
Based in London, THS is comprised of five members
and works across a range of fields spanning music,
fashion, film, motion graphics, advertising and
branding. Renowned for its innovative and highly
thoughtful approach to art direction and design,
the studio has won numerous awards for its work.

Clients and collaborators include Alexander McQueen,
Absolut, BBC, Christian Dior, Nike, Massive Attack,
Mandarina Duck, Lancôme, Nick Cave, Robbie
Williams, Nokia, Grace Jones, Gnarls Barkley,
Solange Azagury-Partridge and The Rolling Stones.

1 Paul Smith/Le Book: Creative directory, 2009
2 Massive Attack: Collected, 2006
3 Prét a Porter Paris: Autumn Winter 2009
4 New York Times: Fifth anniversary cover, in
   collaboration with United Visual Artists, 2009
5 Baibakov: Moscow art gallery, 2008
6 Robbie Willams: Tour logo, 2006
7 Aesir: Mobile phone manufacturer, 2009
8 Money Sevenfifty: Clothing label, 2008
9 Prét a Porter Paris: Fashion trade show, 2008
10 SOPHNET. Clothing label, 2007
11 Stand Off: Magazine logo, 2004
12 Radial: Specialist music service, 2007
13 Paget Baker: PR agency, 2006

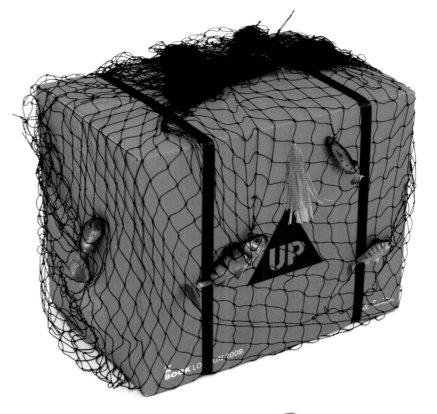

1

2

3

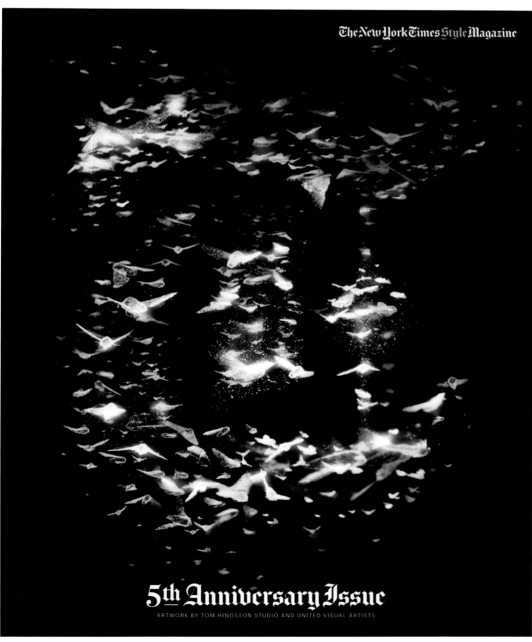

4

BAIBAKOV

5

6

7

8

9

10

11

12

13

Holmes Wood

Studio 27 / 38 Burns Road / London SW11 5GY
T +44 (0)20 7326 9970 / F +44 (0)20 7350 2450
info@holmes-wood.com
www.holmes-wood.com

Management Lucy Holmes, Alexandra Wood
Contact Nicki Oldham
Staff 10 **Founded** 2000

Company Profile

Holmes Wood was founded on a collision of complementary talents in sign and graphic design. We have since become one of Britain's leading designers of direction and information schemes. Our work includes all aspects of wayfinding and signs, identities and print.

Every project is headed by one or both of the principals, Lucy Holmes and Alexandra Wood. We give clients frank and incisive advice as a prelude to design that is original and appropriate. Based in studios near Battersea Park in London, our close-knit team is confident, positive and at ease with handling creative challenges.

Clients range from major galleries, museums and other arts institutions to heavyweight corporate groups, commercial and service organisations. We have won a number of accolades, most recently a Gold Design Effectiveness Award from the Design Business Association for our work at Manchester Art Gallery.

Clients

British Library, British Museum, DSTL, English Heritage, London Transport Museum, Manchester Art Gallery, Natural History Museum, Pitt Rivers Museum, Royal Marsden Hospital, Royal Opera House, Somerset House, Tate Britain, Tate Liverpool, Tate Modern, The National Gallery, Tower of London, University of Westminster, University of Greenwich, V&A Museum, Virgin Atlantic, Westminster City Council, Whitechapel Gallery, Wimbledon School of Art

Awards

Silver D&AD
Gold DBA Design Effectiveness Award

1   Identity for Garden Designer, Fiona Budden
2   English Heritage, Consultation Document
3   Tate International Conference, all design material
4   Manchester Art Gallery, Map Design
5   Manchester Art Gallery, Leaflet Design
6   V&A Museum, Guide Book
7   V&A Museum, Corporate Membership Pack
8   Westminster City Council, Paddington Recreation Ground, Wayfinding, Sign Design and Information Graphics
9   The Natural History Museum, external Wayfinding and Sign Design
10 The historic Albert Dock, Liverpool, Wayfinding, Sign Design and Information Graphics
11 Tate Modern, Wayfinding, Sign Design and Information Graphics
12 Virgin Atlantic, Wayfinding, Sign Design and Information Graphics, Heathrow, Terminal 3
13 The National Gallery, Wayfinding, Sign Design and Information Graphics
14 V&A Museum, Wayfinding, Sign Design and Information Graphics

Fiona Budden
Garden Design

1

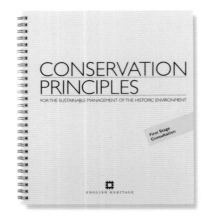

2

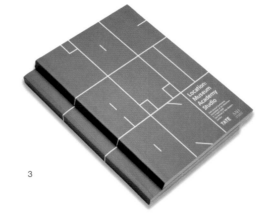

3

4

5

6

7

8

9

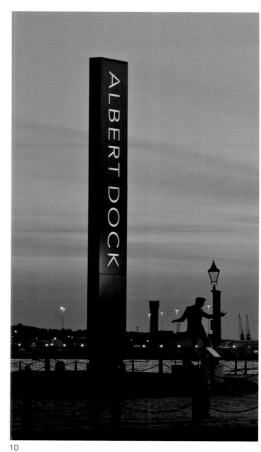

10

11

12

13

14

Jake
Design for the Consumer

Design Studio / Top Floor / 16 Bromley Road /
Kent BR3 5JE
T +44 (0)208 633 3962
hello@jake.uk.com
www.jake.uk.com

Contact Jake

Company Profile
Here at Jake we believe that good design and
marketing solutions should evoke a reaction, it should
sell, inform, excite and inspire. We strive for design
excellence and work closely with our clients to be
marketing partners. We work hard to learn about their
business to make more informed creative decisions
which will enhance their offer, promote its profile and
increase its profits.

Brand Consultants + Environmental Design

Graphics
Identity
Print and Packaging
Environmental
Web

Interiors
Food
Fashion
Services and Retail
Exhibition

beckworth
emporium
FINE PRODUCE | GARDEN NURSERY RESTAURANT

Beckworth Emporium Branding and Retail Interiors

60

Kem Environmental Management Branding and Webdesign

Fitzpatrickreferrals Branding

Eciffo Furniture Branding and Webdesign

Fitzpatrickreferrals Branding and Webdesign

Sogaro Milano

Isis Bottled Water Branding and Packaging

Thomas Cook Branding and Retail Interiors

BAEC Marketing Direct Mail Campaigns

Channel Islands Co-operative Branding and Retail Interiors

Harrods Award Winning Interiors

KIWI Branding development

Kiosk
Design & Art Direction

The Site Gallery / Brown Street / Sheffield S1 2BS
T +44 (0)208 144 5908 (Skype™)
david@letskiosk.com
www.letskiosk.com

Company Profile
Based in Sheffield UK, with like-minded collaborators working remotely, Kiosk is a design studio founded in 2005 and creatively led by ex-Designers Republic designer David Bailey

Clients
Arts Council England
BBC
Coca Cola
Condé Naste Publishing
Dance4
Drum&BassArena
Futuresonic
Just-b. Productions
Gatecrasher
GCI London
Marshall Cavendish
Ministry Of Sound
Mother
Nickelodeon
Polydor
Sheffield Contemporary Arts Forum
Sheffield Hallam University
Universal Music
V2 Music
Warner Music

1 SOYO, Sheffield
2 The Automatic, Steve McQueen & This Is A Fix
3 Various Artists, Print Is Dead
4 Futuresonic 2009
5 Union Jack, Pylon Pigs
6 nottdance08

1

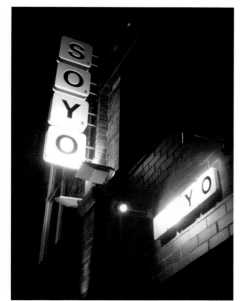

3

2

4

nottdance08
17–26 October

6

5

LAW Creative
An Integrated Marketing Communications Agency

LAW Creative – London
Ninety Long Acre / Covent Garden / London WC2E 9RZ
T +44 (0)20 7849 3035

LAW Creative – Harpenden
Four Waterside / Station Road / Harpenden
Hertfordshire AL5 4US
T +44 (0)1582 469300 / F +44 (0)1582 460050
brett.sammels@lawcreative.co.uk
www.lawcreative.co.uk

Management Nicola Ellis, Managing Director
Brett Sammels, Client Services Director
Keith Sammels, Creative Director

Founded 1999

Company Profile
Our creative work is tailored to chosen markets and
communicates the core promise. We are able to work
on the planning and implementation of complete
campaigns or, alternatively, on a project-by-project
basis, to attack specific areas where revenue is lacking
and will benefit from a tailor-made/cost effective
communications response.

We're easy to work with and we know what works.
We'll give you plenty of ideas, but when you know
what you need, we'll do it! We're not cheap, we're not
expensive, but we'll always try to ensure the numbers
add up for the person paying the bill.

Services
Creative Concepts / Branding / Graphic Design
Promotion & Advertising / Interactive
Account Handling / Project Management
Specialist Food & Lifestyle Photography
Display Graphics / Research / Media Buying

Clients
Amida Spa
Caffè Nero
Caffè Ritazza
Crowne Plaza
Compass Group
David Lloyd Leisure
G Casino
Grosvenor Casinos
Harbour Club
Holiday Inn
IHG
Mecca Bingo
Next Generation
Royal Veterinary College
Streamline Foods
The Gore Hotel
Threshers Group
Weight Watchers

Lisa Tse Ltd
Creative Consulting

Gresham House / 24 Holborn Viaduct /
London EC1A 2BN
T +44 (0)207 2489 248 / F +44 (0)207 9909 248
design@lisatse.com
www.lisatse.com

Management Lisa Tse, Creative Director
Contact Lisa Tse
Staff 10 **Founded** 2005

Company Profile
CREATIVE INTELLIGENCE
Lisa Tse Ltd is a creative agency founded by
international designer and businesswoman Lisa Tse.
Our studio provides a multidisciplinary design service
harnessing pure design with thoughtful intelligent
details.

More than just a design studio, we are a creative
think tank that can create, refresh and sustain your
business to realise its full potential.

With a focus on fresh perspectives and forward
thinking, we adopt a creatively driven approach that
supports companies in a diverse commercial capacity
across the globe.

See also Packaging Design p. 132

1 China Now: A Retrospective
   China Design Now spread
2 China Now: A Retrospective
   Far East Film Festival spread
3 China Now: A Retrospective
   A selection of spreads
4 Twice Fashion Accessories Poster
5 Twice Fashion Accessories Website
6 Twice Fashion Accessories Brochure
7 Twice Fashion Accessories Storefronts
8 Twice Fashion Accessories Campaign Visual

1

2

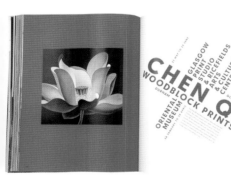

4

5

6

7

8

Magpie Studio

2 The Hangar / Perseverance Works /
38 Kingsland Road / London E2 8DD
T +44 (0)20 7729 3007
hello@magpie-studio.com
www.magpie-studio.com

At the heart of everything we do is a belief that the right idea should not only engage its audience, but also deliver the message. From one man bands to orchestras, we've been there – and not only got the t-shirt but designed it too.

After several years of experience working at some of London's top design agencies, Magpie Studio was formed by three founding partners with the common goal of solving communication problems with great ideas, beautifully crafted.

Small but perfectly formed, our approach is hands on, working with a wide range of clients – of varying shapes and sizes.

Our Clients include
Action on Addiction, All Change, Arts Aimhigher, The Delfina Foundation, Gavin Martin Associates, GDR Creative Intelligence, Knight Frank, Land Securities, Logica, Royal Mail Stamps and Collectibles, Royal Mint, Silverlining Furniture, Tate Britain, University of the Arts London, The Women's Institute.

To find out more, or to see our work in more depth, visit our website or call us on the number above.

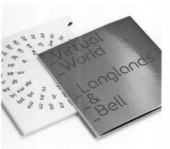

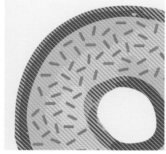

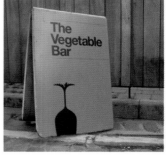

Make
Brand Studio Ltd

504B The Big Peg / 120 Vyse Street /
Birmingham B18 6NF
T +44 (0)845 456 9592
studio@wearemake.com
www.wearemake.com

Management Benjamin Ridgway, Director
Contact Benjamin Ridgway, Brand Development
Staff 3 **Founded** 2003

Company Profile
We are Make, a passionate and productive brand
studio based right in the middle of the UK. We have
been established for 5 years and in this time have
helped numerous clients develop strategies and
brand identities giving them the ability to market their
business effectively in today's competitive market.

Our wide range of in-house skills means that our
clients can benefit from strong brand continuity
throughout all of their marketing strategies. Our
key areas of expertise are brand identity, strategy,
positioning, Flash presentation, web development,
exhibition, animation and mobile content.

Currently we are working closely with Birmingham
City University, assisting them with the growth of their
brand identity and raising awareness through highly
creative marketing campaigns.

Whether we are working for a small start up or
with a large multinational, two common threads run
intertwined through all our work: our love for what
we do, and the effort we put into creating something
previously unseen.

If you want to talk to us about your marketing please
get in touch, and let's Make it happen.

Clients
Birmingham City Council
Dudley City Council
Birmingham City University – Acting Department
Birmingham City University – Media Department
Birmingham City University – Health Department
Chetwoods Architects
TK Maxx
Solaris Botanicals
Ten4 Magazine (Channel 4)
Lovell Homes
NHS
The National Skills Academy
Brights And Stripes Baby Wear

1 DVD Showeel Packaging Design
  Birmingham City University
  Acting Department
2 08/09 Theatre Programme
  Birmingham City University
  Acting Department
3 09 Summer School Print Campaign
  Birmingham City University
  Acting Department

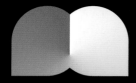

Make/
We/Define/Brands
Print/Digital/Environment

BrandDevelopment/Web/Interactive/Mobile/
Product/BroadcastTV/Film/Print/Corporate
Presentation/BrandedEnvironments

See Portfolio/
www.wearemake.com

Studio Phone/
T/ +44 (0)845 456 95 92

Email Enquiries/
studio@wearemake.com

DVD/09 Showreel/
Birmingham City
University

08.09/ Programme/
Birmingham
School of Acting

Summer Brochure/
Birmingham City
University

Multistorey

Studio 10 / 51 Derbyshire Street / London E2 6JQ
T +44 (0)20 7729 8090
us@multistorey.net
www.multistorey.net

Contact Harry Woodrow
Founded 1997

Company Profile

Multistorey are London-based art directors and designers. Partners Rhonda Drakeford and Harry Woodrow founded Multistorey in 1997 after graduating from Central Saint Martins.

We work with clients across industries ranging from fledgling fashion and furniture labels to multinational corporations. Our very broad ranging portfolio includes art direction, branding and identity, packaging, exhibition and events, retail design and shop fit, print for books, brochures and invitations, advertising campaigns and websites. Our personal, egalitarian approach to design ensures all clients, large or small can expect focused attention from our creative team.

Each brief is a new challenge, with unique problems that demand their own specific solutions. Strong ideas and a considered, functional response are core to all Multistorey's projects. We pride ourselves in creating work that is surprising, exciting and beautiful. Our passion for production and process are integral to the development of the end product. We enjoy collaborating and experimenting with a broad range of printers and craftspeople: from laser etchers to knitters and weavers.This allows us to produce innovative results, within any size budget.

We believe that design plays an important role in society, and that it should never be lazy. Our work aims to be accessible to all, irrespective of their level of visual training — design elitism is not for us. Increasingly, we endeavour to make our solutions as environmentally sensitive as possible, which in no way restricts our creativity, it only makes life more interesting.

1-4   Lyric Hammersmith
      London theatre. Branding, art direction, design and signage.
5-6   Nokia Prism Collection
      Sales brochure for a group of mobile phones. Art direction and graphic design.
7-8   AV Festival 08
      Digital arts festival in the North-East of England, with the theme of "Broadcast". Branding, art direction, design and copywriting.
9-10 Constructive Lives
      West London interiors store. Branding, art direction, graphic and interior design and exterior tiled cladding.

1

2

3

4

5

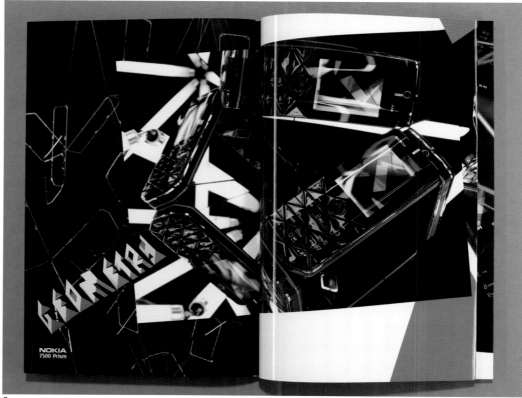

6

7

8

9

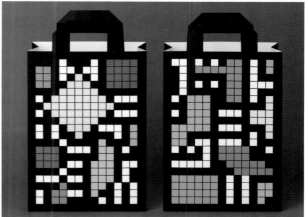

10

N1 Creative Ltd

Unit 3 / 11-29 Fashion Street / London E1 6PX
T +44 (0)20 7655 4321 / F +44 (0)20 7655 4575
info@n1creative.com
www.n1creative.com

Management Jacky O'Leary, Gavin Mackie
Contact Jacky O'Leary
Staff 15 **Founded** 2001

Company Profile
N1 is a brand and communications agency.
Our reputation for innovation, creativity and
responsiveness means that we deliver something
fresh and new on time, every time.
N1 delivers results.

What we excel in
Brand generation and activation across:
– Communications
– Environment
– Packaging
– Online and digital

What makes us tick
– Integrity
– Innovation
– Relationships
– Culture
– Results

Clients
N1 embraces diversity which is demonstrated through
our work across a broad range of sectors and
organisational size. Our clients include:
Bausch & Lomb
BBC Club
Ben & Jerry's
Emerging Markets Private Equity Association
European Environment Agency
Gartner
Maximuscle
Merchant Navy Training Board
Network Rail
Royal Netherlands Embassy, London
Sainsbury's
Savant Healthcare Ltd
South West RDA
UK Commission for Employment and Skills
UK Trade & Investment
University of Surrey
World Health Organisation

Awards
We are multi-award winning, with awards spanning
all areas of our expertise.
Our awards include:
Gold Mobius Award
DBA Design Effectiveness Award
B2B Marketing Award
Clarion Award
IMA Top 10 Digital Agency
W3

Results

Sales exceeded first year projections by 125%

DBA Design Effectiveness Award

eates
d love

37°
thirtysevendegrees

Welcome

Results

Opening gym membership exceeded plan by 60% with subsequent gym expansion.
Gold Mobius Award

n1

NewEdge + The Brewery
End to end innovation

18 Petersham Road / Richmond / London TW10 6UW
T +44 (0)20 8439 8400 / F +44 (0)20 8439 8410
london@newedge-thebrewery.com
www.newedge-thebrewery.com

Management Paul Stead, Co CEO
Pam Henderson Ph.D., Co CEO
Contact Paul Stead
Staff 50

Company Profile
NewEdge + The Brewery brings you a new type
of consultancy.

Award-winning design combines with business
strategy and disruptive research to deliver powerful
new approaches to growth through brand, packaging,
product and environmental solutions.

We've worked with many of the world's largest
brands through to some of the smallest start ups.
In every case we challenge you to think differently,
disrupt the norm and uncover attractive opportunities.

Call us for a strategic approach to design and
innovation that delivers outstanding business results.

Left Brain + Right Brain
Logic + Creativity
Growth + Innovation
NewEdge + The Brewery

Clients
Air Products
Boeing
Colgate-Palmolive
DSM
DuPont
Eastman
Ferrari
John Deere
Kellogg
Microsoft
Molson Coors
Motorola
Procter & Gamble
Solae
Waterstone's
Weyerhauser

**See also Packaging Design p.136 and Interior,
Retail and Event Design p.204**

Creating winning opportunities

Branding of an exclusive club to increase advocacy and
loyalty amongst existing members, drive new membership
and improve its appeal.

Objective

Objective Studio / The Courtyard / 17 West Street /
Farnham / Surrey GU9 7DR
T +44 (0)1252 718 400 / F +44 (0)7092 844 589
hello@objectivestudio.com
www.objectivestudio.com

Management Carl Groth, Alastair Pope
Contact Carl Groth
Staff 6 **Founded** 2005

Company Profile
We are a brand communications studio that
formulates brand strategy, develops identities
and implements creative solutions across print,
web, packaging, exhibitions and events.

We work with a diverse range of innovative
brands creating original, relevant and memorable
communication solutions.

Our mission is to ignite our client brands and inspire
their customers.

Our services include
Branding
Communication
Corporate Identity
Exhibition
Design for Print
Packaging
Digital / Online / Web
Retail / POS

Clients
Best Friends Pet Products
Butlins
Cosmopolitan
Guinness Partnership
Jabra
Johnson & Johnson
KatDC
Maximuscle
Noetica
Option
Pervasic
Piz Buin
Porcelanosa
Portal Partnership
Red Bull Racing
Sealion Shipping
Sovereign
Wallstreet
Yell

1   Elias Topping - Identity creation
      and brand development
2-3   Butlins - Brand implementation
      and format design
4-5   Johnson & Johnson - Exhibition stand for
      cosmetic treatment product range, Evolence
6-10   Best Friends Pet Products - Brand development
      and packaging design for the TastyBone range
      of dog food and play products

1

2

3

4

5

6

7

8

9

10

ODD

12-14 Berry Street / London EC1V 0AU
T +44 (0)20 7490 7900 / F +44 (0)20 7681 1688
info@thankodd.com
www.thankodd.com

Management Simon Glover, Nick Stickland
Contacts Simon Glover, Nick Stickland
Staff 12 **Founded** 2002

Company Profile
ODD is a design-led communications agency based
in London.

Established in 2002, we have become a Design Week
Top 100 agency and built relationships with clients in
the UK and across the globe.

Our award-winning portfolio combines design and
strategy to create interactive, engaging campaigns
that influence consumers perceptions, emotions and
behaviour.

The team at ODD draws on experience from many
disciplines: architecture, advertising, digital,
product and graphic design. We pride ourselves
on incorporating this mix of skill-sets into every brief
and place as much value on working collaboratively
as we do creatively.

Clients
Armani, Bacardi, Boots, Coca Cola, Diageo, Evisu,
Grohe, H&M, Kaupthing, Kerrang!, Kickers, Kiss,
Lee Cooper, Lend Lease, Mitchells and Butler,
New Look, Nokia, Nike, O2, Oxfam, PlayStation,
Red Bull, Reevoo, Sony, Uniqlo, Westfield, WGSN

Awards
OneShow Interactive Awards 2008
Bronze, Integrated Branding Campaign

Event Awards 2008
Winner, Unique Visitor Attraction

Event Awards 2008
Finalist, Best use of a Blank Canvas Space

European Design Awards 2007
Merit, Stationary Design

European Design Awards 2007
Finalist, Brand Identity

D&AD Awards 2007
Nominated, Brand Identity

Design Week Awards 2006
Winner, Retail Innovation

Images from left:
Zacapa Rum Brand Launch
Brandcast.tv Brand Identity
NIKEiD Studio London Launch
Sony Colour Rooms Interior Design
The End/AKA Club Marketing
Uniqlo Menswear Catalogue
Uniqlo UT Promo Material
Greenwich Peninsula Retail Brochure
Lend Lease Retail Brochure
A Night of Vision invitation for Lend Lease
Kickers POS & Advertising
Casarotto & Ramsey Associates Identity/Website
GDR Global Innovation Report
Evisu Collection Catalogue
Westfield London Launch Invite

NIQLO
ENS-
EAR
2009

UT
UNIQLO
TOO MANY T-SHIRTS.

Shops, cafes, bars and restaurants

Bluewater
Golden Square
The Meadows
Overgate
Touchwood
Bridgefie
Chelmer
Clarence
Eastbour
Elephant
Park Plac
Tithebarn

Greenwich Peninsula

Lend Lease

A Night of Vison

LOVE THY KICKERS

Lend Lease

Casaro
Ra
sso

GDR
CREATIVE
INTELLIGENCE

31 Global Innovation Report January 2009

ORB Creative

Studio 209b / The Big Peg / 120 Vyse Street /
Birmingham B18 6NF
T +44 (0)870 220 2648
info@orbcreative.com
www.orbcreative.com

Management Robert Bloxham
Contacts Anthony Jones, Robert Bloxham
Founded 2004

Five years ago, a crack commando unit was sent to prison by a military court for a crime they didn't commit. They promptly escaped from a maximum security stockade to the Birmingham underground. Today, still wanted by the government, they survive as soldiers of fortune. If you have a problem, if no one else can help, and if you can find them, maybe you can hire... The ORB Team.

Expertise
Graphic Design
Branding
Illustration
Web Design
Advertising
Digital Marketing & Strategy
Exhibitions

ORB CREATIVE Presents

DESIGN H

ORB Creative Presents A Noodle Arms Production "DESIGN HARD II"
Starring Max Bikeman James Chopper Sissy Balloon Brian 'The Kong' Swing and The Birmingham Zom
Washing Up by Ben Bubbles Location Research by Ant E Pod Bad Language by Mac The Mouth Official movie soundtrack
© ORB Creative Productions 2009. "Rocket" supplied by Noodle Arms 2009.

IN ASSOCIATION WITH

 www.orbcreative.com

RD II

Parent

Brand exploration & design / Print design / Online

5 Park Place / North Road / Poole / Dorset BH14 0LY
T +44(0)1202 717 333
mail@parentdesign.co.uk
www.parentdesign.co.uk

Contact Chris Harman
Founded 2003

Company Profile
Parent is a creative boutique specialising in brand design, direction and exploration, print design and online solutions.

We work direct with clients, with advertising and media agencies and have been known to develop our own projects and brands.

Over the passed 6 years we have successfully forged working relationships with clients across diverse sectors from fashion and pr, to finance, publishing, property, travel, media and entertainment.

Our focus is to develop original creative solutions that are appropriately targeted for your business, whether that be directed at urban youth or boardroom level.

marc wallace

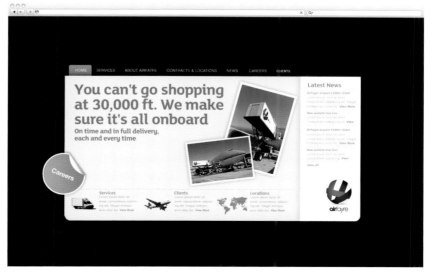

...IT outsourcing

Pencil

Unit 8 / Westfield Court / Third Avenue /
Westfield Ind Est / Midsomer Norton /
Somerset BA3 4XD
T +44 (0)845 290 3930
info@penciluk.co.uk
www.penciluk.co.uk

Staff 3 **Founded** 2008

Company Profile

We are a team of creatives who believe that using pencil & paper to scamp out ideas is the starting block of design. Great design starts with a spark of creativity, which then, with hard work, and an eye for detail is crafted into something special.

We pride ourselves on building strong relationships with our clients and this is key to our success. We work for a wide variety of companies in many different sectors, but approach all with the same objective; to create something which communicates their strengths and personalities and delivers effective results.

1 Forever Green
2 Bath & North East Somerset Council
3 Eclipse Retail Furniture
4 Ray Watkins Photography
5 LaceLock
6 Rock & Road
7 Wittenstein Aerospace – Computer Software
8 Skills Provision Recruitment Agency

1

2

3

4

SECURE SHOELACE FASTENING SYSTEM

5

6

8

7

REINVIGORATE Ltd
Total Brand Experience

Kestrel Court / Harbour Rd. / Portishead /
Bristol BS20 7AN
T +44 (0)800 500 7090 / F +44 (0)800 500 7091
martin@reinvigorate.co.uk
www.reinvigorate.co.uk

Management Founder & 2 Board Directors
Staff 12 **Founded** 2003
Contact Martin Monks

Company Profile
Reinvigorate is a Brand Design and Project
Management agency. We can provide a complete
'Turn Key' solution; from Brand positioning and
communication through to delivery and installation
of a Brand's in-store experience. Reinvigorate can
deliver a total brand experience from the creation
and conception of the brand through to the full
brand experience in store.

We have the capabilities and expertise to deliver
profitable business solutions for any brand in any
format from stand alone or a concession; through
to single free standing units in a third party store.
In addition to designing the brand experience we
also Project Manage the installation and construction
of the full retail environment within the client's
specified budget.

Clients
Adams Childrenswear
Brooks Brothers
Brantano
Ermes
Hallmark Cards
Jacques Vert
Jawad Business Group
Moda in Pelle
Pixi Beauty
Planet
Things Accessories
Terra Plana

See also Interior, Retail and Event Design p. 206

See also Interior, Retail and Event Design p. 206

1 Brooks Brothers
   Flagship Store – London, UK
2 Moda in Pelle Ltd
   Flagship store – Leeds, UK
3 PLANET
   New concept store – London, UK

1

94

2

3

things*

PLANET

moda in pelle

Uⴄ UNITED NUDE ™

Pearsons
Department Stores

pix!

TERRA PLANA

REINVIGORATE
RETAIL DESIGN AND BUILD

Sedley Place Ltd.
www.sedley-place.co.uk

68 Venn Street / London SW4 0AX
T +44 (0)207 627 5777 / F +44 (0)207 627 5859
info@sedley-place.co.uk
www.sedley-place.co.uk

Management Mick Nash
Contacts Rupert Denyer, Alastair Patrick
Staff 30 **Founded** 1978

Company Profile
Sedley Place is an independent design agency.
Our skills are diverse: from brand strategies to graphic
design, product design to premium packaging, interior
and architectural design to digital media.

We have offices in London and Edinburgh and we
work with businesses and organisations of all sizes
all over the world.

At Sedley Place, you'll find empathy and intelligence.
We offer a potent mix of traditional craftsmanship
and leading technology, art and design, precision
detailing and grand scale vision. We pride ourselves
on our ability to provide original creative solutions that
surprise and delight.

Simply put, we build desire.

Branding and graphic design
Our branding and graphic design services include:
- Brand strategy
- Brand and identity design
- Printed materials
- Typography
- Stamp design

In a world of narrow product and service
differentiation, the way in which a brand is brought to
life is more important than ever. We use our proven
Cornerstone Methodology to help us differentiate our
clients' brands from their competitive set, delivering
actionable insight, inspiring ideas and integrated
solutions. We ensure the end result is crafted
beautifully, communicating its message in the most
appropriate tone of voice.

Clients
The Gleneagles Hotel
Cumbria Tourism
Shaftesbury Young People
The Royal Mail

**See also Packaging Design p. 146, New Media
Design p. 174 and Interior, Retail and Event
Design p. 208**

Shaftesbury Young People

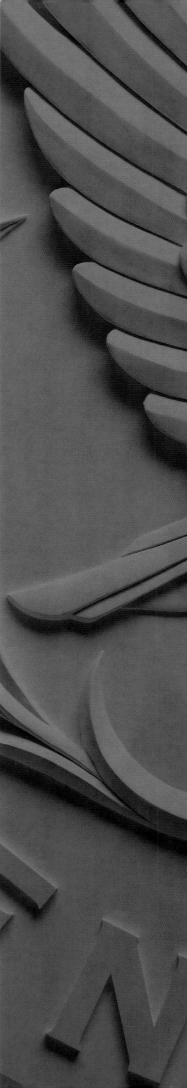

Stocks Taylor Benson Ltd
Graphic Design
Consultancy

1 Grove Court / Grove Park / Leicester LE19 1SA
T +44 (0)116 240 5600 / F +44 (0)116 240 5601
trevor@stbdesign.co.uk
www.stbdesign.co.uk

Management Joe Bakowski, Managing Director;
Glenn Taylor, Managing Creative Director;
Darren Seymour, Client Service Director;
Trevor Flannery, Sales & Marketing Director
Staff 30 **Founded** 1988

Company Profile
Stocks Taylor Benson is a straightforward graphic
design agency that produces design for packaging,
POS and literature. We realise that graphic design
is about solving problems and the only reason we
are working with our clients is for our design work
to directly, or indirectly, generate a greater income
for them.

When our clients work with us they deal directly with
designers, allowing them to get straight to the point.
Our clients have found that this ensures the most
efficient account management and the best
creative delivery.

Our aim is to provide, at all times, excellent design,
excellent value and, above all, excellent service.

Clients
Antalis
Arjowiggins
Avon
Beiersdorf
Black & Decker
bmi
DEWALT
Herbalife
Interflora
Julian Graves
Kingston Technology
Kitchen Craft
Morrisons
Next
Office Depot
Sainsbury's
Tesco
Wilkinson

packaging

literature

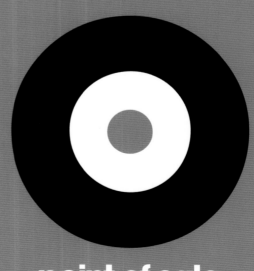

point of sale

STOCKS TAYLOR BENSON

graphic
design
experts

unlike most other design companies we try to keep it simple:

no bullshit

no bag carriers, just straightforward, to the point, graphic design & artwork.

Substrakt
Creative Communication

Studio 39 / Fazeley Studios / 191 Fazeley Street /
Digbeth / Birmingham B5 5SE
T +44 (0)121 224 7422
team@substrakt.co.uk
www.substrakt.co.uk

Management Andy Hartwell, James Braithwaite
Contact Claire Hartley
Staff 6 **Founded** 2006

Company Profile
Substrakt helps clients communicate their ideas and
ethos through a variety of media, including brand
development, web design and print.

Clients
BBC
Channel 4
Selfridges & Co
CABE
Birmingham City University
DTZ
Microsoft
Tesco
RIBA
Cushman & Wakefield
Walkit.com

See also New Media Design p. 176

Maybird is changing.

Re-launching Saturday 15th November

With several famous brands arriving in time for Christmas, 850 free car park spaces, on-site amenities for cyclists, new easier access off the Birmingham Road and open late 7 days a week, Maybird is a different kind of shopping park.

MAYBIRD
SHOPPING PARK
www.maybirdshopping.co.uk

JCDecaux

mama
feel
good!

Microsoft®
XNA
GameCamp

X48

game.Run();

I WANT THE CHANCE TO FEEL PAMPERED.

IT'S MY BIRTHDAY PARTY AND I DON'T KNOW WHAT TO WEAR.

I NEED A NEW SUIT FOR AN IMPORTANT BUSINESS EVENT, BUT DON'T KNOW WHERE TO START.

I JUST DON'T KNOW WHAT SUITS ME ANYMORE !

LOVE THYSELF

SELFRIDGES&Cº
www.selfridges.com
BIRMINGHAM

jobplot
grow your creative career

substrakt
creative communication

YOU ARE INVITIED TO JOIN US IN CELEBRATING THE LONG AWAITED SUBSTRAKT HOUSEWARMING PARTY

meshedmedia

BIG SCREEN BIRMINGHAM

TAK!
Art, Design & Development

Studio 204 / The Custard Factory /
Birmingham B9 4AA
T +44 (0)121 288 2528
studio@taktak.net
www.taktak.net

Management Dom Murphy, Neil Kinnish
Contact Dom Murphy, Creative Director
Staff 7 **Founded** 2004

Company Profile
An independent creative team of graphic designers, art directors and programmers.

Always considered, our work ranges from quirky brand identities to large art archives and everything in between. In all cases, our work shares the same values; unique simple ideas.

Our expertise in concept, design and programming allows us to deliver a complete brand experience—both online and off—ensuring consistency across all media.

We provide our clients with a unique and diverse difference with well designed, well built and occasionally, award winning work.

If you would like a copy of our latest promotional materials simply email us and we'll do the rest.

Clients
Ikon Gallery
Birmingham Museums & Art Gallery
Deaf Cultural Centre
Arts & Business
Red Bull
Clarks Originals
Intel
HSBC
Topshop
Marketing Birmingham
Thomas Tallis School
British Dance Edition

Awards
SXSW 2004 Winner (Arts)
SXSW 2006 Finalist (Eduction)
Webby Official Honoree 2006 (Eduction)

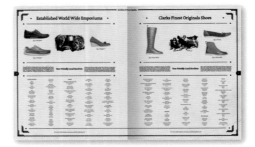

British Dance Edition 2010 branding

Ikon Gallery website

Walkie Talkie magazine for Clarks Originals

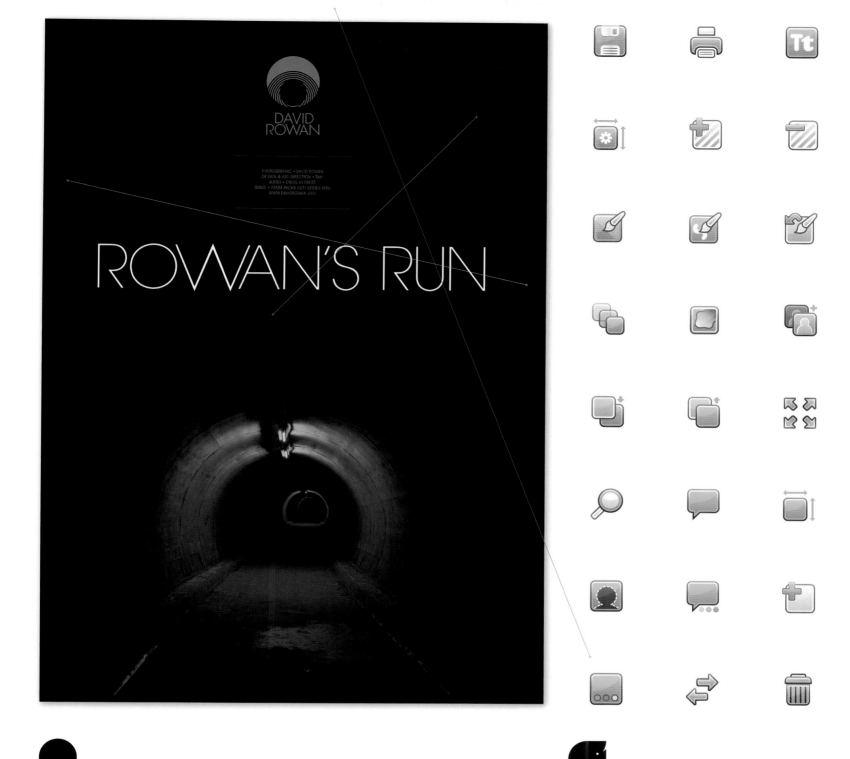

David Rowan promotional materials

Poky logo & mascot

Walkie Talkie logo

Colourbox logo

Play With pictures application icons

David Rowan logo

taniemedia®

68 Great Eastern Street Ground Floor /
London EC2A 3JT
T +44 (0)20 7739 2762 / F +44 (0)20 8082 5361
contact@taniemedia.com
info@taniemedia.com
www.taniemedia.com

Management Stefanie Ambrois de Pascarella
Contact Thibault Rigoulet
Staff 14 **Founded** 2005

ABOUT US / OUR STORY

We believe in the positive power of brands.
Brands colour our world.
They can dazzle and annoy – or they can inspire.
We believe the best brands play a role in improving
how people see themselves and how the world
sees them.

We have a wider perspective.
We're based in London, but we're a diverse bunch.
We bring an international flair to our work. While we
understand British design, you'll hear French and
Spanish flying around our office as much as English.
We wouldn't have it any other way.

SERVICES

Mixed media…expanding branding.
What drives us is creating memorable brand
experiences. But we don't pluck them out of the air.
Nor are they formed in some creative vacuum,
isolated from reality.

The brand is boss.
Your brand's core values underpin our creative work.
Together, we can create a new brand identity, evolve
what you have, or simply use established guidelines
to create gorgeous new experiences.

STRATEGY

We can always turn out beautiful work.
But truly memorable experiences succeed through
their strong strategic grounding.

**Brand audit – Brand definition – Brand positioning
– Brand exploration – Brand architecture**

IDENTITY

Great brands have great personalities.
People get to know and trust them – even identify
themselves with them. Identity unites all the external
factors to create a unique brand essence.

**Naming – Visual identity – Verbal identity – Sonic
identity – Motion identity – Guidelines – Brand
launch – Brand spaces – Packaging – Online –
Broadcast design**

- Art Network
- Ask Models by Schwarzkopf
- Barens Chocolat
- Eutelsat
- Thema
- Value Retail
- Solaris
- Tooway
- Qooljets
- Sloane Essentials
- Long Tall Sally

taniemusic. **tanie**media. **tanie**space.

branding by design

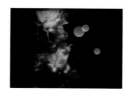

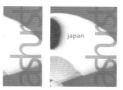

Taxi Studio

93 Princess Victoria Street / Clifton / Bristol BS8 4DD
T +44 (0)117 973 5151 / F +44 (0)117 973 5181
alex@taxistudio.co.uk
www.taxistudio.co.uk

Management Alex Bane, creative services director/
partner; Spencer Buck, creative director/partner;
Ryan Wills, creative director/partner
Contacts New Business Enquiries,
alex@taxistudio.co.uk;
Recruitment Enquiries, terry@taxistudio.co.uk
Staff 10 **Founded** 2002

Company Profile
We build relationships. That may sound emotive,
but for us, it's simply what effective communications
should do.

Whether it's the relationship between your brands
and those who buy them, your company and the
people who work for it, or your business and its
shareholders, we're here to help you hook up, get
better acquainted and develop something really
really special.

Here's a bunch of Brand Identities – hallmarks of our
creativity. More can be found at www.taxistudio.co.uk

Clients
Beverage Partners Worldwide
Clarks
The Coca-Cola Company
Diageo
The Edrington Group
Paradigm Services
Science Museum
Tesco
Willie's World-Class Cacao

Awards
We've won over 100 national and international awards
including: D&AD, Design Week, Communication Arts,
and the New York Festivals Grand Award for Design.

**See also Packaging Design p.148 and New Media
Design p.178**

1   Merlyn is an essential part of the England Cricket
    Team's practice sessions. It's a magical machine
    that simulates the world's best spin bowlers with
    stunning accuracy
2   A refreshing, relevant logo for King Water Koolers
3   Adding value to the visual and verbal language of
    Adlib (a leading creative recruitment company) via
    a new logo and strapline
4   Helping Kilver Studio (a professional dance studio)
    get off on the right foot
5   A name and logo for a new toilet cleaning device
    that, um, squeaks
6   Knowle DGE (Discovery / Guidance / Enjoyment)
    was our proposal for a school of children with
    learning difficulties
7   Helping an oversized shoe retailer stand above
    the crowd. It was a runaway success – sales were
    up 40% in the first week
8   Devising a deliciously simple, flexible branding
    system for Willie Harcourt-Cooze's exquisite
    range of cacao products
9   A logo for a creative award scheme that
    demonstrates creativity
10 Paradigm provide secure communications to
    the MOD. When they briefed us to create their
    identity, we were all ears
11 An identity and motto for Sidcot Quaker School.
    When we presented this idea to the Governors,
    it literally sailed though
12 Eva Kecseti makes beautiful, bespoke leather
    handbags. We made a beautiful, bespoke identity
    from her initials

1

2

3

4

5

6

7

8

9

10

11

12

Tijuana

71 Queens Road / Bristol BS8 1QP
T +44 (0)117 910 2440
info@tijuanadesign.com
www.tijuanadesign.com

Management Tony Stiles, Howard Swift
Staff 5 **Founded** 2001

Company Profile
We enjoy clearly and consistently communicating
great ideas for our clients.

Clients
Bristol Old Vic, Cheltenham Festivals,
Encounters Festival, Larmer Tree Festival,
Music Beyond Mainstream, NESTA, Organix,
Parlophone, Soil Association, Sustrans

Some examples of our work in print
(on walls) and online (on screens).

Turquoise

Suite G First Floor Holborn Hall /
193–197 High Holborn / London WC1V 7BD
T +44 (0)20 7831 2803 / F +44 (0)20 7430 9838
hello@turquoisebranding.com
www.turquoisebranding.com

Company Profile

We create strategy, brand identity and motion branding. We believe that every business, every person, and every brand should be the best they can be. We love crystal clarity, outrageous ambition and making things better. That's why we set up, and it's why we're still enjoying ourselves.

Our Services

Strategy
Brand Identity
Motion Branding

Expectations

Clarity, Creativity, Commitment, Contribution

Clients

Arab Media Group
Arab Television & Radio Network
BBC
Buongiorno
Channel 4
Claro
Creative Edge
Deloitte
Design Council
DIFC
Du
Dubai Customs
Dubai Holding Group
ENOC
Feather & Black
Freedom 4
ITV
Maltacom
MBR Foundation
Pipex
SAGIA
Saudi TV
Skills 4 Industry
Saudi Telecom
Telenet
UPS

STC - Hardware Packaging

STC - Fleet Livery

STC - Pre Pay Cards

STC - Global Brand System

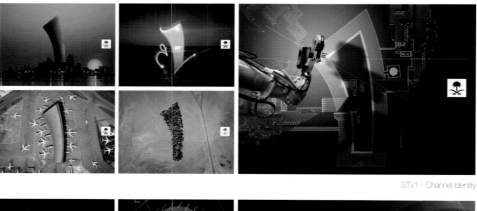

STV1 - Channel Identity

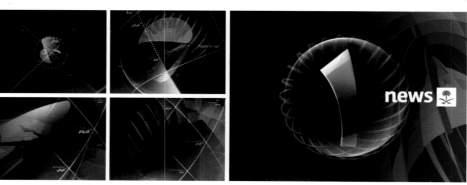

STV1 News - Programme Identity

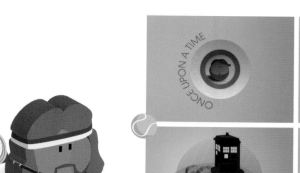

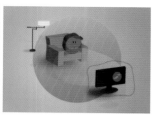

BBC - Information Film

Go - Sim Card

Go - Monthly Magazine

Go - Brand Marque

du - Brand Marque

du - Brand Guidelines

du - Brand Manual

du - Fleet Livery

du - Hardware Packaging

Two by Two
Design Consultants Ltd

348 Goswell Road / London EC1V 7LQ
T +44 (0)207 278 1122 / F +44 (0)207 278 1155
zebra@twobytwo.co.uk
www.twobytwo.co.uk

Management Salvatore Cicero, Ashwin Shaw
Contact Ashwin Shaw
Founded 1995

Company Profile
Care more
Risk more
Explore more
Expect more

We are brand identity and strategy specialists.
We create and interpret brands, bringing them
to life across any medium you care to choose.

Packaging. POS. Literature. Direct Mail.
Exhibitions. Interiors. Websites.

Clients
Agua Fabrics
Biotherm
Cottages to Castles
CPM Interiors
Design Art London
Elemis
Europcar
In Harmony
La Roche Posay
L'Oreal Professionnel
Nicole Farhi
Opus Magnum
Pexhurst Services
Purelogicol
Ralph Lauren
Redken
Royal Mint
Task Systems
Tisserand
Verco
Vichy

Awards
Gold Best in Metal Awards
Winner Food and Drinks Awards
Winner Health and Beauty Salon of the Year
Winner Professional Beauty Salon of the Year
Finalist Design Week Awards
Finalist Design Effectiveness Awards
Best New Male Fragrance Packaging
Fragrance Foundation Awards 2006

(PURELOGICOL)
Brand creation and packaging range

(AGUA)
Brand creation, corporate collateral, website design
and build

(CPM)
Brand creation, corporate collateral, website design
and build

purelogicol
purifying
facial cleanser
daily care
FREE FROM PARABENS, ALCOHOL, COLOURS AND PERFUME
FOR ALL SKIN TYPES
purelogicol
super antioxidant
moisturiser
daily care
FREE FROM PARABENS, ALCOHOL, COLOURS AND PERFUME
purelogicol
clarifying
facial toner
daily care
FREE FROM PARABENS, ALCOHOL, COLOURS AND PERFUME
FOR ALL SKIN TYPES

CPM/Interiors

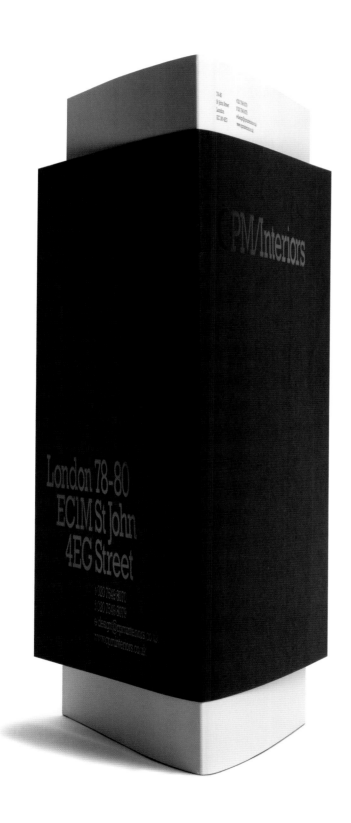

Wildwood Creative
Brand & Design
Consultancy

Capital Tower / 91 Waterloo Road / London SE1 8RT
T +44 (0)20 7928 4343 / F +44 (0)20 7928 1144
info@wildwoodcreative.co.uk
www.wildwoodcreative.co.uk

Contact Andrew Murray

Company Profile
Wildwood Creative is a London based design agency
with clients all over the UK and internationally.

We specialise in designing, producing and
implementing the full range of design communications.
Whether you're looking to create a new brand,
or develop an existing one, we can help.

Every business can benefit from good design, which
is why over the years we've delivered many successful
projects for a broad range of organisations, ranging
from small and medium-sized enterprises to global
corporations.

So now you know a little bit about us, we'd love to
hear more about you.

Clients
Aviva Investors
British Land
DP Aromatherapy
Jones Lang LaSalle
Lancôme
Land Securities
Optomen Television
Quinlan Private
Strutt & Parker
Westminster Council

1 Wimbledon Tennis Lettings: Advertising, Branding,
  DM & emailers, Signage, Stationery, Website
2 The Bentall Centre Kingston, Aviva Investors:
  Branding, Investment document, Marketing
  collateral, Photography, Print, Production
  management
3 DP Aromatherapy: Branding, Emailers, Marketing
  collateral, Product photography
4 Munroe K Asset Management: Advertising, Brand
  identity, Brand guidelines, Marketing collateral,
  3D modelling, Website
5 P&P Songs: Branding, CD packaging, Marketing
  collateral, Stationery
6 People Resourcing: Brand identity, Photography,
  Stationery, Website

Munroe K

Merry Christmas

4

5

P&P

people resourcing

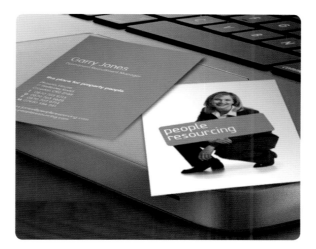

6

CHICKEN PIE £4.25

STEAK PIE £4.25

+ MU

FRES

PACKAGING
DESIGN

The Brand Union
The Global Brand Agency

11-33 St John Street / London EC1M 4AA
T +44 (0)20 7559 7000 / F +44 (0)20 7559 7001
info@thebrandunion.com
www.thebrandunion.com

Contacts Dave Brown, UK Chairman
Glenn Tutssel, Executive Creative Director
Jonny Westcar, Managing Client Director

Company Profile
The Brand Union is a world-class global brand
agency, comprising 500 people across 21 offices.
What binds us together is a deep-seated commitment
to becoming masters of the art and science of brand
building. In all our disciplines, Brand Mastery is our
central organising thought.

We help brands grow. We offer direction. We protect
brands against the economic and cultural elements.
Bright ideas guide us – they are the lifeblood of our
business. And we take pride in crafting and shaping
the brightest ideas into memorable and valuable
brand worlds.

We have created identities for some of the world's
leading brands including American Express, Absolut
and Bank of America.

We have delivered product branding and brand
environments for clients such as SABMiller,
Masterfoods, Unilever, Motorola and Diageo.

And we have helped grow and position corporate
giants like Canon, Credit Suisse, Corus, Deloitte and
Vodafone.

Our services include Research, Strategy, Design,
Engagement and Evaluation.

To buy or not to buy. More than just the box your
product comes in, your packaging is a multi-sensory
experiential form of advertising that can be the key
decider in your customer's choice.
At The Brand Union, we know there is no better
way to cut through at the point of purchase and
communicate your product's values and those of your
brand. The Brand Union has worked with a number of
global brands, and we know that the moment of truth
for multi-million pound campaigns is the final three
feet when the consumer makes the ultimate buying
decision. Our design delivers impact at 30 feet and
engagement at three feet, so that when that moment
comes, the consumer believes in your brand.

Clients
Bacardi
Mars
Reckitt Benckiser
SABMiller
Vodafone

**See also Branding and Graphic Design p. 24 and
New Media Design p. 162**

DESIGN TO ECLIPSE OTHER BRANDS

Bulletproof

28-32 Shelton Street / Covent Garden /
London WC2H 9JE
T +44 (0)207 395 3636 / F +44 (0)207 395 3737
debbie@wearebulletproof.com
www.wearebulletproof.com

Management Gush Mundae, Jonny Stewart,
Nick Rees, Melissa Smith
Contact Debbie Inman, Head of New Business
Staff 32 **Founded** 1998

Company Profile
Bulletproof solves business problems, intelligently,
strategically and creatively…for global brands through
to small entrepreneurial startups.

We believe design can change the world (or at
least improve the bottom line) and we take an
IMC-informed approach to ensure our work speaks
with one compelling voice and a consistent graphic
language across the brandscape.

We specialise in three core areas of design:
1) branding 2) packaging and 3) shopper marketing.

We are large enough to tackle any task, but small
enough to stay true to our entrepreneurial founder-
culture of conviction, integrity and energy.

Our difference is our people. We are a multi-talented,
multicultural bunch who are constantly driven to
better our best work. Bulletproof always delivers
fantastic ideas, executed creatively by a team who
really care.

Clients
The Coca-Cola Company
Kraft Foods
GlaxoSmithKline
Sainsbury's
HJ Heinz
Beam Global Spirits & Wine

we are: strategic, independent, informed, creative, ambitious, lovely, intelligent, progressive... Bulletproof

Dairylea
Packaging strategy
Branding
Packaging graphics –
across 40 packs
NPD
Copywriting

Design Activity

Beech House / 6 St Pauls Road / Clifton /
Bristol BS8 1LT
T +44 (0)117 933 9400 / F +44 (0)117 923 9989
andrew.stroud@design-activity.co.uk
www.design-activity.co.uk

Management Andrew Stroud, MD
Contacts Andrew Stroud, Pat Starke
Staff 15 **Founded** 1994

Company Profile
Design Activity is a privately owned branding and
packaging design agency with more than 15 years
experience of working with national and international
clients.

During this time we have established our reputation
around two key factors:

A unique mix of people – a range of talent and
experience with the right combination of attitude and
application.

A wide-ranging category experience – enabling us
to bring innovation, inspiration and a new perspective
to creative projects.

We use this expertise to create considered and
effective design solutions across the disciplines
of Packaging Design, Branding & Communication
and Point of Sale materials.

Ultimately, our greatest influence is in the in-store
environment where our experience allows us to
deliver relevance and visibility to brands at the point
of purchase. The success of our clients remains
a true testament to the effectiveness of our work.

design activity

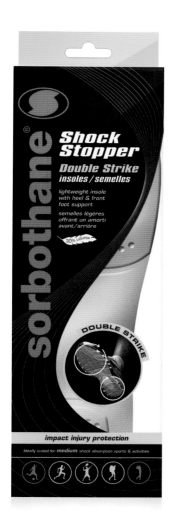

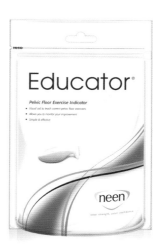

jones knowles ritchie

128 Albert Street / London NW1 7NE
T +44 (0)20 7428 8000 / F +44 (0)20 7428 8080
info@jkr.co.uk
www.jkr.co.uk

Contact Andrew Knowles
Founded 1990

Company Profile
There are 30,000 items in the average supermarket,
yet only 20 items go into the average shopping
trolley.

To succeed, your brand needs to get noticed and
chosen. We know how. Perhaps that's why, in a
category down 6%, drench sales have grown 66%.

Clients
Diageo
Mars
Molton Brown
Premier Foods
Unilever
United Biscuits

Awards
Gold DBA Effectiveness Award 2008 – Molton Brown
Silver DBA Effectiveness Award 2008 – Stella Artois

100% clean

Kinneir Dufort
Design Strategy
Innovation Brand

5 Host Street / Bristol BS1 5BU
T +44 (0)117 901 4000 / F +44 (0)117 901 4001
susanna.clasby@kinneirdufort.com
www.kinneirdufort.com

Management Jim Orkney
Contacts Susanna Clasby, Sean Devane
Staff 45 **Founded** 1977

Company Profile

Kinneir Dufort is one of the world's most experienced and versatile innovation and design companies which, for over 30 years, has been delivering intelligent, creative solutions that help clients achieve business success.

We operate internationally with clients and projects in North America, mainland Europe and the Far East, as well as in the UK, working with global corporations and brands as well as SME's and entrepreneurs.

Our growing, 45-strong team delivers innovation and design programmes in diverse categories including: healthcare, food and drink, home and personal care, consumer goods, industrial products, telecommunications and social networking.

Our approach, which is centred on an understanding of both the user-experience and the client's business needs, brings together the elements of innovation in a comprehensive process which incorporates: research, ideation, product, packaging and graphic communications design, user interface and human-factors, engineering, prototyping and early-stage manufacture.

Kinneir Dufort's reputation for excellence and quality is backed up by ISO 9001: 2008 and ISO 13485: 2003 (medical device design) certification.

Awards

Recent awards: 2008 DBA Design Effectiveness and 2009 Red Dot Product Design

Images

Structural design for cooking oils, CJ Korea

Gro Clock, Gro Company

Hospital bedside cabinet, Bristol MaidTM. Part of the Design Council's Design Bugs out initiative

Structural design for mineral water, CJ Korea

Accu-Chek Aviva Nano, blood glucose monitor. Red Dot design award winner 2009

reddot design award
winner 2009

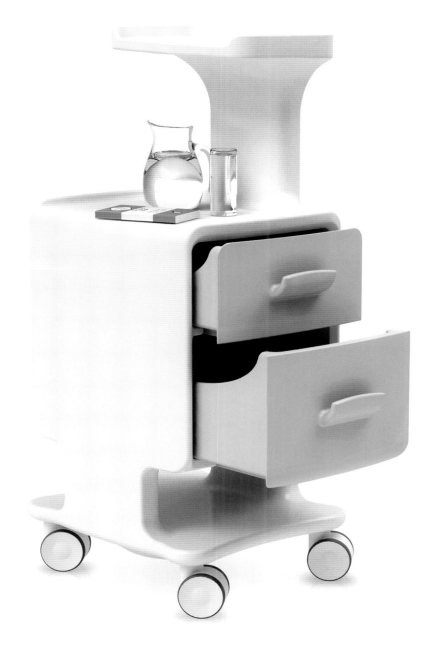

Lisa Tse Ltd
Creative Consulting

Gresham House / 24 Holborn Viaduct /
London EC1A 2BN
T +44 (0)207 2489 248 / F +44 (0)207 9909 248
design@lisatse.com
www.lisatse.com

Management Lisa Tse, Creative Director
Contact Lisa Tse
Staff 10 **Founded** 2005

Company Profile
CREATIVE INTELLIGENCE
Lisa Tse Ltd is a creative agency founded by
international designer and businesswoman Lisa Tse.
Our studio provides a multidisciplinary design service
harnessing pure design with thoughtful intelligent
details.

More than just a design studio, we are a creative
think tank that can create, refresh and sustain your
business to realise its full potential.

With a focus on fresh perspectives and forward
thinking, we adopt a creatively driven approach that
supports companies in a diverse commercial capacity
across the globe.

See also Branding and Graphic Design p.68

See also Branding and Graphic Design p.68

1 TAP'NY water bottle and collar label
2 TAP'D NY bumper stickers
3 TAP'D NY bottle front and rear showing branding
   and message
4 TAP'D NY range of messages

1

"WORKING WITH LISA TSE LTD IS ONE OF THE BEST BRAND DECISIONS WE'VE MADE."

CRAIG ZUCKER, CEO, TAP'D NY

2

3

4

LPK
London

93-95 Gloucester Place / Suite G3 / London W1U 6JQ
T +44 (0)20 7487 8251 / F +44 (0)20 7487 8477
cathy_lowe@lpk.com
www.lpk.com

Contact Cathy Lowe
Founded 1983

Company Profile
LPK is an international design agency with a proven track record in Building Leadership Brands. By integrating strategy, design and innovation, LPK transforms relevant consumer, shopper and market insights to create value, sustain leadership and transform businesses.

Our portfolio of category-leading brands and long-term client relationships attracts some of the best and brightest creative minds. The combination of strategic skills, creative disciplines and cross-cultural perspectives results in brand-building innovation across media, geography and time.

With a presence in Europe, North America and Asia, LPK is the world's largest employee-owned brand design agency.

Services
Brand Strategy
Idea Generation
Brand Identity
Packaging Design
Product Design
Retail Activation
Marketing Communications
Research and Analysis
Motion/3D
Trends

Clients
3M
Always
Cadbury
CPW
Flash
Gillette
Hasbro
Jim Beam
Kellogg's
Mr.Propre
Nestlé
Olay
Pampers
Pringles
Swiffer

Building Leadership Brands®

NewEdge + The Brewery
End to end innovation

18 Petersham Road / Richmond / London TW10 6UW
T +44 (0)20 8439 8400 / F +44 (0)20 8439 8410
london@newedge-thebrewery.com
www.newedge-thebrewery.com

Management Paul Stead, Co CEO
Pam Henderson Ph.D., Co CEO
Contact Paul Stead
Staff 50

Company Profile
NewEdge + The Brewery brings you a new type
of consultancy.

Award-winning design combines with business
strategy and disruptive research to deliver powerful
new approaches to growth through brand, packaging,
product and environmental solutions.

We've worked with many of the world's largest
brands through to some of the smallest start ups.
In every case we challenge you to think differently,
disrupt the norm and uncover attractive opportunities.

Call us for a strategic approach to design and
innovation that delivers outstanding business results.

Left Brain + Right Brain
Logic + Creativity
Growth + Innovation
NewEdge + The Brewery

Clients
Air Products
Boeing
Colgate-Palmolive
DSM
DuPont
Eastman
Ferrari
John Deere
Kellogg
Microsoft
Molson Coors
Motorola
Procter & Gamble
Solae
Waterstone's
Weyerhauser

**See also Branding and Graphic Design p.80 and
Interior, Retail and Event Design p.204**

Creating breakthrough opportunities

A ground breaking wine preservation product supported
by considered packaging and a unique delivery system,
creating distinction and stature.

Osborne Pike

22 Circus Mews / Bath BA1 2PW
T +44 (0)1225 489269 / F +44 (0)1225 469633
brandstories@osbornepike.co.uk
www.osbornepike.co.uk

Management Steve Osborne, David Pike,
David Rivett
Contacts Steve Osborne, David Pike,
Lulu Laidlaw-Smith
Staff 10 **Founded** 2002

Company Profile

Our clients describe us as 'a big agency in a small
package', combining excellent strategy and creativity
with speed, close collaboration and cost-effectiveness.

Our mission, our passion and our process are one
and the same: we tell brand stories through brand
identity and packaging design.

Your brand story is all you have. We make it our
business to understand it, to feel it, and then to tell
it in the most compelling way we can imagine.

Clients

Sara Lee Corporation
Kraft Foods Europe
Heineken
Beam Global
Beverage Brands
Hildon
Tracklements

every brand has its story...

High Pavement / The Lace Market /
Nottingham NG1 1HN
T +44 (0)115 9476 444/555 / F +44 (0)115 9504 948
david.rogers@pure-equator.com
www.pure-equator.com

Management Sue Allsopp, Managing Director;
David Rogers, Creative Partner
Staff 22 **Founded** 2000

Company Profile
Pure Equators passion is:
Blue Sky Thinking within Bottom Line Budgets;
As you pay for talent not rent

Why Pure Equator?
GLOBAL THINKING
International Brand Portfolio

ON BRAND
Passionate about creating and nurturing brands

REPUTATION
Revolutionary & Multi Award Winning

RESULTS FOCUSED
Thorough understanding of what our clients
want to achieve

STRATEGIC KNOWLEDGE
In-depth knowledge of the markets

OUR ACCOUNT TEAM
Total commitment to your needs

LIBERATING CREATIVITY
Finding the right solution

Clients
Aldi, Associated British Foods, Bausch & Lomb,
Blockbuster, Boots The Chemists, Fox's Confectionery,
Gordon Ramsay, Label M, Lypsyl, Roald Dahl, Tesco,
Toni & Guy, Trevor Sorbie, Volvo CE

Awards
Pure Equator is proud to have won multiple design
awards for creative and commercial excellence.
Winners and Gold Statuette's including:
London International, New York Festival, Pure Beauty,
Creativity Annual Awards, Mobius, Cream Awards

1 My World Website. Created just for children,
   this fully interactive site combines information,
   downloads, quizzes and competitions, teaching
   children to respect the earth in a fun and
   imaginative environment.
2 My World Brand and Packaging. A Children's
   Lifestyle Brand. Imaginatively teaching our future
   generation to respect the planet. Innocent, fairytale
   tones, capturing the very essence of childhood.
3 Blockbuster Popcorn. Iconic 1950's style imagery
   reflecting the heyday of cinema, with humorous
   characterisation designed to engage the consumer
   through personality.
4 Blockbuster Snacks. Snacks packed with
   personality, with humorous copywriting forming
   the basis for these scrummy looking packs.
5 Tesco Roald Dahl Cakes. Effectively partnering
   a super power in imagination and a retail giant.
   Maintaining the magic was paramount for this
   licensed partnership.
6 Roald Dahl Style Guide. Brand Guidelines to the
   World of Roald Dahl, this comprehensive style
   guide captures the very essence of the brand and
   promotes a cohesive approach across all mediums.

 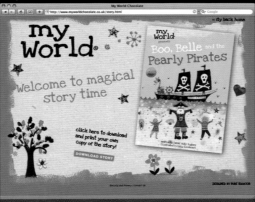 

"From conception through to completion, PureEquator exceeded my expectations throughout the entire design process for My World. Passionate, creative, proactive and reactive, the whole team believed in the project. Launching a brand is a long journey, PureEquator made it a pleasurable one."
– Brand Manager, My World

BLOCKBUSTER
MOVIE MATI
HE LOOKED
BLOCKBUSTER
MOVIE MATI
SHE WAS WOWED
BLOCKBUSTER
MOVIE MATINÉE
HE SURPRISED HER WITH
SALTED POPCORN!

"David Rogers immediately understood our vision for the Blockbuster brand and interpreted
the brief perfectly. Our new Popcorn and Snack designs have exceeded all expectations.
The creativity of PureEquator is second to none and working with David is a real pleasure"
– Brand Manager, Blockbuster

"David Rogers and his team at PureEquator worked wonders on bringing together a collection of ideas and theoreticals to create a powerful design that captured aspects of both the Roald Dahl and Tesco brands. The result has been an immensely successful range of innovative cakes in beautiful packaging. I look forward to the opportunity of working with David again.
Senior Product Development Manager, Tesco

"It's all about Dahl – Brand guardians to the WORLD OF ROALD DAHL. This comprehensive style guide captures the very essence of the brand and promotes a cohesive approach across all mediums. When creating this guide, we got deep inside the way Roald Dahl expressed his vision, achieving a faultless story from conception to finished product. To create a style guide for such an iconic symbol of creative literature was an inspiring journey.
David Rogers, Creative Director

Sedley Place Ltd.
www.sedley-place.co.uk

68 Venn Street / London SW4 0AX
T +44 (0)207 627 5777 / F +44 (0)207 627 5859
info@sedley-place.co.uk
www.sedley-place.co.uk

Management Mick Nash
Contacts Gerry Barney, Alastair Patrick
Staff 30 **Founded** 1978

Company Profile
Sedley Place is an independent design agency.
Our skills are diverse: from brand strategies to graphic
design, product design to premium packaging, interior
and architectural design to digital media.

We have offices in London and Edinburgh and we
work with businesses and organisations of all sizes
all over the world.

At Sedley Place, you'll find empathy and intelligence.
We offer a potent mix of traditional craftsmanship
and leading technology, art and design, precision
detailing and grand scale vision. We pride ourselves
on our ability to provide original creative solutions that
surprise and delight.

Simply put, we build desire.

Packaging design
Over the past 30 years we have worked with the
worlds premium products and drinks brands,
helping to bring many new brands to the market
place and setting new standards for the sector.
Our work for Smirnoff and Johnnie Walker has
helped add value and pioneer new markets for
these international brands.

Brands
Johnnie Walker
Gordons
Tanqueray
Grant's
Cardhu
Chivas Regal

See also Branding and Graphic Design p. 96,
New Media Design p. 174 and Interior, Retail and
Event Design p. 208

JOHN WALKER & SONS

JOHNNIE
Blue!

A BLEND OF OUR VERY

BLENDED SC

DISTILLED

ER & SONS

ESTD. 1820
KILMARNOCK SCOTLAND

JOHN WALKER & SONS

PRODUCT OF S

Taxi Studio

93 Princess Victoria Street / Clifton / Bristol BS8 4DD
T +44 (0)117 973 5151 / F +44 (0)117 973 5181
alex@taxistudio.co.uk
www.taxistudio.co.uk

Management Alex Bane, creative services director/
partner; Spencer Buck, creative director/partner;
Ryan Wills, creative director/partner
Contacts New Business Enquiries,
alex@taxistudio.co.uk;
Recruitment Enquiries, terry@taxistudio.co.uk
Staff 10 **Founded** 2002

Company Profile
We build relationships. That may sound emotive,
but for us, it's simply what effective communications
should do.

Whether it's the relationship between your brands
and those who buy them, your company and the
people who work for it, or your business and its
shareholders, we're here to help you hook up, get
better acquainted and develop something really
really special.

Here's some of our latest pack designs
– a taster of our creativity. More can be found
at www.taxistudio.co.uk

Clients
Beverage Partners Worldwide
Clarks
The Coca-Cola Company
Diageo
The Edrington Group
Paradigm Services
Science Museum
Tesco
Willie's World-Class Cacao

Awards
We've won over 100 national and international awards
including: D&AD, Design Week, Communication Arts,
and the New York Festivals Grand Award for Design.

**See also Branding and Graphic Design p. 106 and
New Media Design p. 178**

1 Following a much needed redesign our solution
   raised sales (making lots of dough for Tesco)
2 A product that delivers exactly what it says on
   its pocket sized packs. Inside, two individually
   wrapped, tempting and delectable squares of
   dark chocolate (also designed by Taxi) reward the
   consumer. Consistently selling out in stores across
   the country is rather rewarding for Willie. As for our
   reward… well, just re-read the previous sentence
3 Knobbly Carrot soups stood out from the rest but
   their packs didn't stand out on the shelves. We
   added a hyphen to create an eccentric aristocratic
   Welsh family spanning six generations and made
   them Masters of Organic Foods

Relationships involve flours.

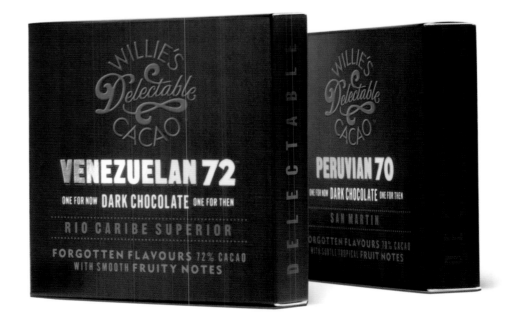

Delicious premium chocolates.

And tasty meals for two.

Alex Bane WLTM like-minded, adventurous types.
alex@taxistudio.co.uk +44 (0)117 973 5151

threebrand

Boat 1502U / The Shore / Leith / Edinburgh EH6 6QW
T +44 (0)131 454 2030
campbell@threebrand.com
www.threebrand.com

Management
Campbell Laird, Nick Cadbury, Gary Fortune-Smith
Contact Campbell Laird
Staff 15 **Founded** 2004

Company Profile
Quite simply we help companies create distinctive
brands

Clients
Aunt Bessie's
Baileys
Baxters
Bushmills
Compass Box
Findus
Heineken
Johnnie Walker
Philips Automotive
Smirnoff

threebrand

Z3 Design Studio
Brand Creation

Studio 2 / Broughton Works / 27 George Street /
Birmingham B3 1QG
T +44 (0)121 233 2545
www.designbyz3.com

Management Richard Hunt, Scott Raybould
Contacts Richard Hunt, Scott Raybould
Staff 6 **Founded** 1992

Design+Realisation
Creating desire through innovation, communicating
through design. We provide integrated highly visible
campaigns in all mediums. Campaigns that inspire,
engage and create desirability for your brand.
Our experience spans the corporate and public
sectors, the arts, music industry, packaging and
leisure industry. View our creative output on-line
www.designbyz3.com

Clients
Sarah Chapman London
Wild Organics
Thinkhappy
Organic Surge
Umberto Giannini Hair Cosmetics
Simple (Accantia Health & Beauty Ltd)
Boots plc
Spa Isha
New Balance
Vicon Motion Systems
Sony Music Entertainment
Warner Music
Birmingham City University
Museum of Modern Art Oxford
University of Warwick

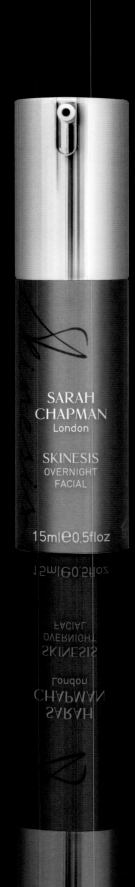

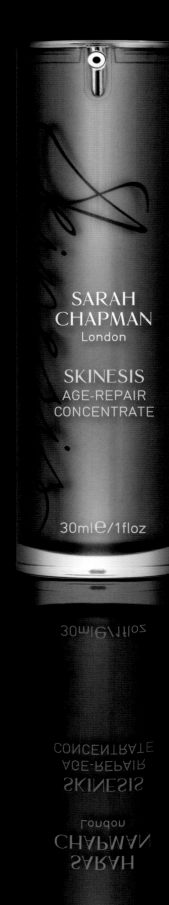

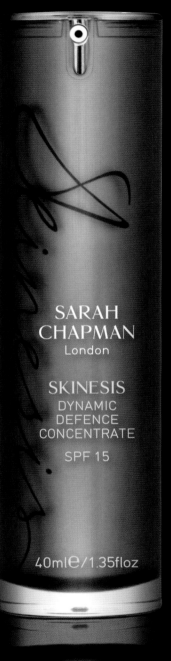

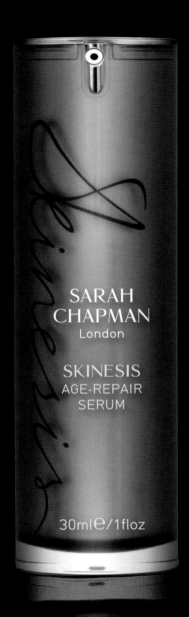

SARAH
CHAPMAN
London

SKINESIS

DYNAMIC
DEFENCE
CONCENTRATE

SPF 15

40ml℮/1.35floz

SARAH
CHAPMAN
London

SKINESIS

AGE-REPAIR
SERUM

30ml℮/1floz

SARAH
CHAPMAN
London

SKINESIS
EYE
RECOVERY

15ml℮0.5floz

SARAH
CHAPMAN
London

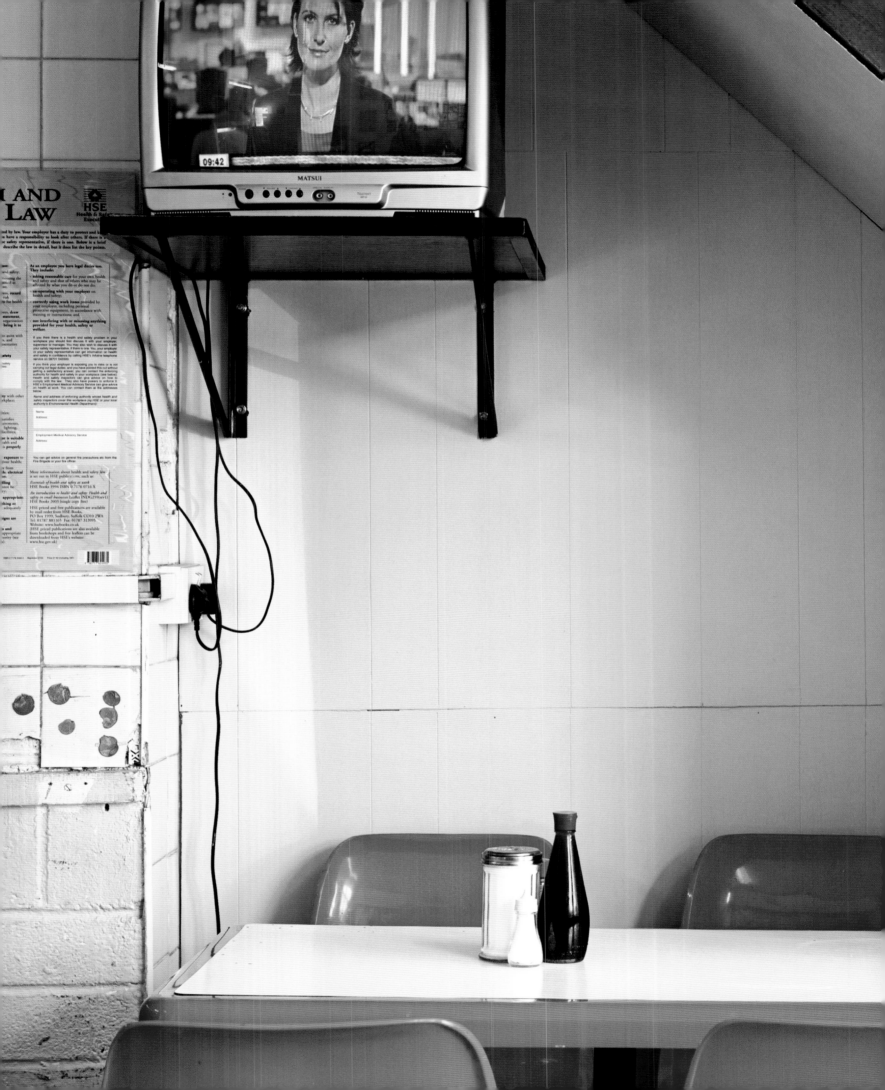

THERE IS
MORE SEATING
AVAILABLE
UPSTAIRS

NEW
MEDIA
DESIGN

The Adhere Creative
Website and New Media Design

Studio 34 / Fazeley Studios / 191 Fazeley Street /
Birmingham B55SE
T +44 (0)121 2850529
info@theadherecreative.com
www.theadherecreative.com

Management Karl Binder, Managing Director
Bobbie Bhogal, Director
Contacts Karl Binder, karl@theadherecreative.com
Chris Ivens, chris@theadherecreative.com
Jason Keyse, jason@theadherecreative.com
Kam Bhogal, kam@theadherecreative.com
Staff 6 **Founded** 2006

Company Profile
The Adhere Creative is a Birmingham media agency
specialising in online interactive websites and
software. This includes web design, content and
project management, online video, audio, print design
and digital communication.

We are based in Digbeth in Birmingham's Eastside
Creative Quarter in Fazeley Studios. Our team's
skills include web design, print design and corporate
identity, audio production, flash animation, film
making and editing, illustration and photography.
As well as this we have recently started developing
applications for facebook and the iPhone alongside
our existing web applications.

Clients
Carphone Warehouse
University of Birmingham
Michelin
Birmingham Forward / Future
Monilink
London 2012 Paralympics
Creative Republic
LIBER Europe
Just Say Please
Think Vehicles
Itsourmovie.com

1 Beautiful Brides – Designer Wedding Dress
  Brochure website
2 Sterling Timer Frame Homes – Canadian based
  Wood Cabin designer website
3 Saint Nicolas Place – Historic Kings Norton
  Website for the winner of BBC 2's 2006 Restoration
  Programme
4 Michelin Microsite – Flash based competition
  website for Michelin
5 Packitin – Community website with online videos for
  a 'Quit Smoking' campaign
6 Think Vehicles – Contract Hire and Business Vehicle
  website

1

2

3

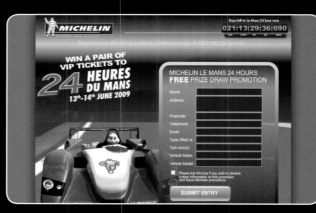

4

5

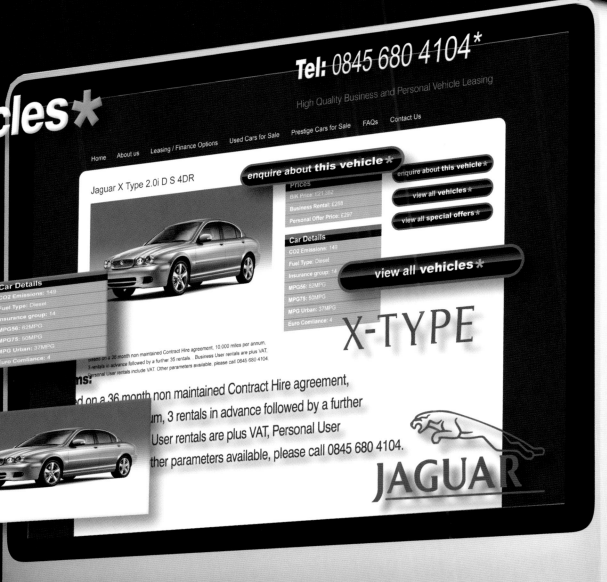

6

Anywhichway

81 Rivington Street / London EC2A 3AY
T +44 (0)20 3178 6380
hello@anywhichway.co.uk
www.anywhichway.co.uk

Contacts David Hopper, Barny Macaulay
Staff 8 **Founded** 2006

Company Profile
Anywhichway was set up in 2006 to offer clients
an alternative, creatively-charged route towards
digital marketing. Our focus was on getting brands
to connect with customers in more interactive and
memorable ways.

Three years on and we've grown into an award-
winning agency powered by highly experienced
strategists, creatives and development experts.
We believe that inspiring businesses is about giving
ideas, insights and strategic solutions that can then
ignite creative results.

We achieve this with a wide range of expertise,
from web design and online marketing to mobile
application development and more. Here's a list
of just some of the skills we offer:

Web design
Advertising
Graphic design
Accessibility
Project management
Usability
Information architecture
Search optimization
Content management systems
Email marketing
Mobile and iPhone apps

Clients
BP
The Climate Group
Channel 4
Just-Eat.co.uk
Magnum/Unilever
NBC Universal
Nizlopi
The Office Group
Octopus Travel/GTA
Orange
Orlebar Brown
Phaidon Press
Robinson McColl
toptable.com

WE CREATE WORK TO MAKE PEOPLE SMILE, SIT UP, TAKE NOTICE, AND START TALKING.

CLIMATE GROUP
EAT SEASONABLY CAMPAIGN

ORANGE
ORANGE UK NEWS

TOPTABLE
TOPTABLE FRANCE LAUNCH

Beef
Digital Thinking & Doing

Unit 4.3 Paintworks / Bristol BS4 3EH
T +44 (0)117 971 1150
hello@wearebeef.co.uk
www.wearebeef.co.uk

Management Kevin Broadley, Tom Burton,
Steve England, Ben Hostler
Contact Ben Hostler
Staff 8 **Founded** 2004

Company Profile
Hello. We are Beef.
We are a creative digital agency.

Creativity is at our heart – we love dreaming up
ideas, solving problems and engaging audiences.
We combine that with strategic thinking, technical
excellence and strong project management to ensure
that what we do delivers the goods.

Our focus is digital but that's not necessarily the first
place we look for inspiration. Answers can appear in
unexpected places sometimes so we make sure we
look there too.

Pop in for tea and let's talk about how we can help
you solve a problem.

Clients
Penguin
Puffin
Jason Bruges Studio
Royal Agricultural College
Sony BMG
Burrell Durrant Hifle
Kid Carpet
Business Link
South West Screen
Watershed
Bristol Media

The Brand Union
The Global Brand Agency

11-33 St John Street / London EC1M 4AA
T +44 (0)20 7559 7000 / F +44 (0)20 7559 7001
info@thebrandunion.com
www.thebrandunion.com

Contacts Simon Bailey, UK CEO
Terry Tyrrell, Worldwide Chairman

Company Profile
The Brand Union is a world-class global brand
agency, comprising 500 people across 21 offices.
What binds us together is a deep-seated commitment
to becoming masters of the art and science of brand
building. In all our disciplines, Brand Mastery is our
central organising thought.

We help brands grow. We offer direction. We protect
brands against the economic and cultural elements.
Bright ideas guide us – they are the lifeblood of our
business. And we take pride in crafting and shaping
the brightest ideas into memorable and valuable
brand worlds.

We have created identities for some of the world's
leading brands including American Express, Absolut
and Bank of America.

We have delivered product branding and brand
environments for clients such as SABMiller,
Masterfoods, Unilever, Motorola and Diageo.

And we have helped grow and position corporate
giants like Canon, Credit Suisse, Corus, Deloitte and
Vodafone.

Our services include Research, Strategy, Design,
Engagement and Evaluation.

Brand experience is a series of interrelated touch
points that imprint a brand in consumers' hearts and
minds. And today, digital design plays a vital part
in providing a channel for consumer input into your
brand, as well as brand expression. A customer's
experience with a brand builds momentum with every
positive interaction and so careful choreography of
this journey is essential.

Digital design is where art and science truly interact
– the science of user experience in search, navigation
and tracking, in combination with the art of beautiful,
relevant and compelling design. Your customer's
experience with your brand builds momentum with
every positive interaction, so careful choreography of
this journey is essential.

Across our services, The Brand Union are strategically
positioned to enhance and build consumer perception
through measurable, cost-effective and engaging
digital design, ultimately helping you build a lifelong
relationship with your customers.

Clients
Argos
Bank of America
Barclaycard
Castrol
Deutsche Post
Learning & Skills Council
Portsmouth FC
Premier League
Rolls-Royce
Vodafone

**See also Branding and Graphic Design p. 24 and
Packaging Design p. 120**

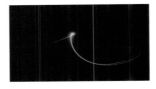

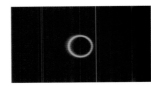

Deviate

BBIC Innovation Way / Barnsley S75 1JL
T +44 (0)1226 720 072
James@WeAreDeviate.co.uk
www.WeAreDeviate.co.uk

Management Adie Flute, Simon Jones, David Winters
Contact James Pearson

Company Profile
Deviate represents good honest northern graft. Smart,
well crafted ideas that work from experienced people
you can trust – but without the Fancy Dan price tags.

Deviate provides a full range of digital design and on
and offline marketing services backed by a straight-
talking approach to brand strategy, research, online
PR, SEO, PPC and social media.

Clients
Universal Studios
Thomson Local
Myprotein
Bosch
Sandals & Beaches Resorts
Experian
Gillette
A4e
Improve Sector Skills Council
Northern Foods
Triumph International
Business Link
Chubb
Duracell
Ernst & Young
Learn Direct
One North East
National Skills Academy for Food & Drink
Skills for Justice
GB Oils
QlikView
Oracle

Deviate

FOUR IV

11 Northburgh Street / London / EC1V 0AN
T +44 (0)20 7336 1344 / F +44 (0)20 7336 1345
simont@fouriv.com
www.fouriv.com

Management Chris Dewar Dixon, Andy Bone,
Simon Thompson
Contact Simon Thompson
Staff 28 **Founded** 1989

Company Profile
FOUR IV is a leading UK based graphic and interior
design agency.

Specialising in brand development and retail & leisure
interior design, FOUR IV is the creative agency behind
some of the world's most exciting and commercially
proven luxury retail and leisure brands.

Currently working in over 14 countries, we are now in
our 20th year.

Clients
Browns
Burberry
Emporio Armani
Dunhill
Dinny Hall
Duchamp
Gas
Gieves and Hawkes
Hawkshead
Kurt Geiger
Liberty
Luella
Mulberry
Thomas Pink
Timberland
American Golf
Boots
DFS
Habitat
Mamas and Papas
Sothebys
Wedgwood
Harvey Nichols
Harrods
John Lewis Partnership
Arnotts
Unitim
Fenwick
Bouwfonds MAB
CBRE
Westfield
Abu Dhabi Tourism Authority
Athenæum
The Grove
InterContinental
Jumeirah Beach
Runnymede
The Langham
Nyonya
First Choice
Carlton Savannah Hotel
Utell

**See also Branding and Graphic Design p. 48 and
Interior, Retail and Event Design p. 194**

One Black Bear
oneblackbear.com

The Old School House / 191 Fazeley Street /
Birmingham B5 5SE
T +44 (0)121 224 7963
info@oneblackbear.com
www.oneblackbear.com

Management Gareth Brown, Richard Elwell,
Jon Harrison, Steve Price, Ross Riley
Contacts rich@oneblackbear.com
gareth@oneblackbear.com
Staff 8 **Founded** 2007

Company Profile
One Black Bear is a specialist digital agency,
concentrating on making all things online the best
they can be.
We work on all levels of budget with both large and
small clients on a retained or project basis.
If there's a problem you need solving or would just
like a cup of tea, give us a call or drop us a mail,
you'll find we're very friendly bears.

Clients
Subaru
Isuzu
Wildfowl & Wetlands Trust
EIC
MADE

Don't just talk to anyone about digital. Talk to a Bear.

The specialists in getting your business working online.

Top Sites

One Black Bear
http://www.oneblackbear.com

ONE BLACK BEAR

Pancentric Digital

4-8 Emerson Street / Bankside / London SE1 9DU
T +44 (0)20 7099 6370
team@pancentric.com
www.pancentric.com

Management Bruce Stewart, James Downes,
Martin Boswell, Simon Fenn

Company Profile
We're a specialist digital agency that combines
creativity, marketing, multi-media and technical
expertise under one roof. We passionately believe
human-centric thinking is the key to more involving
and effective online brand strategies; our end-to-end
solutions are grounded in customer insight.

We work with some of the best-known global brands,
and place great emphasis on client collaboration.
We have extensive experience in insurance, financial
services, entertainment, publishing, FMCG, retail and
pharmaceutical.

We're ranked in the Top 100 design companies by
Design Week and are a Adobe Premier partner.

We're independent and have grown 25% every year
since we were established in 2003.

Main Services
Digital strategy
Branding solutions
User experience
Design & build
Social media
Search, web and email marketing
Innovative media & video

We also offer hosting solutions and own the
Enabler eCRM solution (www.enablermail.com).

Clients
ACE Europe
Allianz/Petplan
AXA Insurance
BBC
Burger King
Cadbury
Chubb
Danone
David Lloyd Leisure
EMI
Fly53
IPC Media
Kerry Foods
Learn Direct
Merck Sharp & Dohme
Muse Developments
Pepsico
Ricoh
RSA
Whitbread

Petplan® Equine

www.yourstables.co.uk

www.petraitgallery.co.uk

www.burgerking.co.uk

www.rsabroker.com/movingstories

www.fly53.com

pancentricdigital

{thinking. people.}

Pixel DNA
DESIGN / ILLUSTRATION / MOTION

Pixel DNA Limited / 32 Wellcarr Road /
Sheffield S8 8QQ
T +44 (0)114 220 2337
info@pixel-dna.com
www.pixel-dna.com

Contacts Marc Tingle, Lucy Warren
Founded 2005

Company Profile
Pixel DNA's services cover a range of design and digital media disciplines. With a wealth of experience in branding and motion graphics, our work attracts clients from a range of industries who come to us because they want an end result that has a high end finish with real visual impact.

Pixel DNA always think about how an idea can be applied across various media. This means that our designs are never flat or one dimensional.

Project Action Stations Title Sequence
Client GMTV

Project Details
A space theme title sequence for a children's ITV program. Each space craft was designed and built from scratch, along with a number of detailed textures. Other elements included composited effects and green screen keying of presenters into animated 3D sets.

Pixel DNA also worked on a number of other pieces including the creation of 'into' and 'out of part breaks', Logo stings, 3D set designs, Flash Website, Printed Literature and Sponsorship Stings.

Client Feedback
"Pixel DNA were highly recommended to me by a colleague and they have certainly lived up to the high praise. Having worked with a number of the larger top London agencies on many previous projects, I can say without hesitation that Pixel DNA are certainly on par when it comes to quality and service.

The work they produce is of an extremely high standard and they continue to deliver fantastic results whilst also exceeding expectations by going above and beyond the brief. They are always very enthusiastic and strive to achieve the best possible end results on time and within budget. Although there is a geographical distance – this has never been an issue, Pixel DNA have always felt like an extension of our own team!

All at GMTV KIDS have been highly impressed with the top quality work that Pixel DNA have produced. Their integrity, creativity and attention to detail has added so much to our project. It's been a pleasure – They've become like family and we look forward to working with them on future projects."
David Kangas / Executive Producer – GMTV KIDS

Clients
ITV
GMTV
Speedo
Lloyds TSB
Sheffield United Football Club
Hilton Hotels
Ministry of Sound
Kidney Research UK
Cancer Research UK
Sheffield Hallam University
Royal Academy of Music (London)
Yorkshire Forward
Lascivious Lingerie
Sheffield International Venues
Fellowes
Stuart Maconie (Radio 1 DJ)

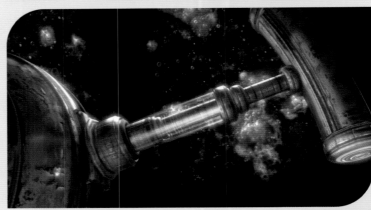
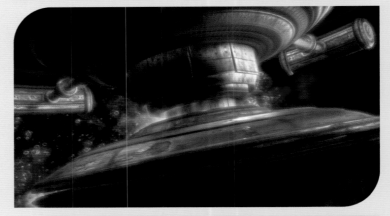

Sedley Place Ltd.
www.sedley-place.co.uk

68 Venn Street / London SW4 0AX
T +44 (0)207 627 5777 / F +44 (0)207 627 5859
info@sedley-place.co.uk
www.sedley-place.co.uk

Management Mick Nash
Contacts David Gardner, Alastair Patrick
Staff 30 **Founded** 1978

Company Profile
Sedley Place is an independent design agency.
Our skills are diverse: from brand strategies to graphic
design, product design to premium packaging, interior
and architectural design to digital media.

We have offices in London and Edinburgh and we
work with businesses and organisations of all sizes
all over the world.

At Sedley Place, you'll find empathy and intelligence.
We offer a potent mix of traditional craftsmanship
and leading technology, art and design, precision
detailing and grand scale vision. We pride ourselves
on our ability to provide original creative solutions that
surprise and delight.

Simply put, we build desire.

New media design
We have a wealth of expertise in both online and
outdoor digital sectors.

Creating motion graphics sequences for spectacular
signs, such as the iconic Coca-Cola sign at Piccadilly
Circus, forms an exciting aspect of Sedley Place's
offer. We are highly experienced in developing a
style of 'visual music', bringing brands to life on
digital screens.

Our knowledge of how to engage audiences is
also applied to create exceptional online brand
experiences. Our services include:

- Website design and build
- Online marketing
- Usability and accessibility services
- E-surveys and market research
- Research, strategy and planning
- Multi-media
- Training
- Copywriting and web-editing

Clients
Coca-Cola Great Britain
The Gleneagles Hotel
The Athenaeum Hotel
The Grove
McKinney Rogers

**See also Branding and Graphic Design p. 96,
Packaging Design p. 146 and Interior, Retail and
Event Design p. 208**

www.gleneagles.com

www.sounessandboyne.co.uk

www.athenaeumhotel.com

Substrakt
Creative Communication

Studio 39 / Fazeley Studios / 191 Fazeley Street /
Digbeth / Birmingham B5 5SE
T +44 (0)121 224 7422
team@substrakt.co.uk
www.substrakt.co.uk

Management Andy Hartwell, James Braithwaite
Contact Tom Martin
Staff 6 **Founded** 2006

Company Profile
Substrakt helps clients communicate their ideas and
ethos through a variety of media, including brand
development, web design and print.

Clients
BBC
Channel 4
Selfridges & Co
CABE
Birmingham City University
DTZ
Microsoft
Tesco
RIBA
Cushman & Wakefield
Walkit.com

See also Branding and Graphic Design p. 100

1 www.jobplot.co.uk
2 www.walkit.com
3 www.substrakt.co.uk
4 www.hareandhoundskingsheath.co.uk
5 www.factoryclub.co.uk

Taxi Studio

93 Princess Victoria Street / Clifton / Bristol BS8 4DD
T +44 (0)117 973 5151 / F +44 (0)117 973 5181
alex@taxistudio.co.uk
www.taxistudio.co.uk

Management Alex Bane, creative services director/
partner; Spencer Buck, creative director/partner;
Ryan Wills, creative director/partner
Contacts New Business Enquiries,
alex@taxistudio.co.uk;
Recruitment Enquiries, terry@taxistudio.co.uk
Staff 10 **Founded** 2002

Company Profile
We build relationships. That may sound emotive,
but for us, it's simply what effective communications
should do.

Whether it's the relationship between your brands
and those who buy them, your company and the
people who work for it, or your business and its
shareholders, we're here to help you hook up, get
better acquainted and develop something really
really special.

Here's two of our recent website creations. Another
good example can be found at www.taxistudio.co.uk

Clients
Beverage Partners Worldwide
Clarks
The Coca-Cola Company
Diageo
The Edrington Group
Paradigm Services
Science Museum
Tesco
Willie's World-Class Cacao

Awards
We've won over 100 national and international awards
including: D&AD, Design Week, Communication Arts,
and the New York Festivals Grand Award for Design.

**See also Branding and Graphic Design p. 106 and
Packaging Design p. 148**

1 www.paradigmsecure.com
2 www.williescacao.com

Purely functional

purely fun-ctional

Universal Everything

T +44 (0)7595 512 975
studio@universaleverything.com
www.universaleverything.com

Management Matt Pyke, Philip Ward
Founded 2004

Company Profile
Working with everything from pencils to generative design, Universal Everything is a diverse studio at the crossover between design and art. With commissions ranging from packaging to stadium events, for clients from Apple to London 2012 Olympics. Our works have shown in galleries from Museum of Modern Art, New York to Colette, Paris.

Motivated by the pursuit of the new, creative research and development are central, leading to self-initiated pieces and unique projects for brands, galleries, collectors and consumers.

Founded by creative director Matt Pyke, we operate as an evergrowing global network of designers, artists, musicians, producers and programmers. From our UK-based studio, we build teams for an approach bespoke to each project.

Since 2004 we have created projects for 41 clients in 23 cities.

Clients
Apple
Sony Playstation
Nokia
Vodafone
MTV Worldwide
Channel Four
Warp Records
George Michael
London 2012 Olympics
Adidas
Nike
Uniqlo
Audi
Renault
Manhattan Loft Corporation
Victoria & Albert Museum, London
Museum of Modern Art, New York

1 www.universaleverything.com
2 MTV Global Rebrand

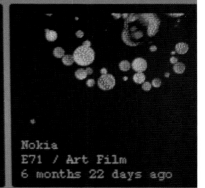

Warp.net
Website
2 months 28 days ago

Designing Seeds
Software-Based Works
4 months 29 days ago

Henderson
Realtime videowall
5 months 22 days ago

Nokia
E71 / Art Film
6 months 22 days ago

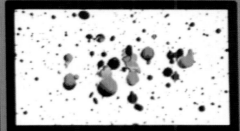

an Loft
y Website
s 14 days ago

V&A Magazine
Article
9m 21d

Universal Everything
2008 Showreel
1 year 1 month ago

Lovebytes
Identity / 2008
1 year 2 months ago

MOMA NYC
Design & the Elast...
1 year 2 months ago

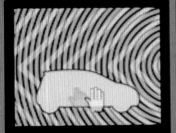

Renault Twingo
Online Campaign
1y 11m 4d

The Guardian
Top 50
1y 11m 4d

AIGA magazine
Processing feature
2 years ago

Grafik 100
Early Works
2y 1m 23d

Peacocks Amongst The...
Wallpaper exhibition
2 years 2 months ago

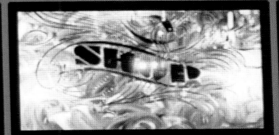

I.D Magazine
Top 40
2y 7m 2d

George Michael
Stadium Visuals
2y 7m 24d

Vodafone
TV Advertising
2y 8m 15d

Shop Advertising
Video Art for Head Office
2 years 8 months ago

Gr
Ex
2 y

ago

Cola
ising
24d

Apple.com
Documentary
3 years 2 months ago

Freefarm.co.uk
Website
3 years 2 months ago

Science Mu...
Installation
3y 4m 27d

manhattanloft.co.uk
Website
3 years 5 months ago

Loveby
2006 F
3 year

SPECIAL
2x BACON 2x SAUSAGES
FRIED BREAD, EGG,
BEANS, TOMATOES
TOAST x2
TEA/COFFEE
£4.00
PLATTER
3x BACON 2x SAUSAGES
2x EGGS, FRIED BREAD
BEANS, TOMATOES
TOAST x2
TEA/COFFEE
£5.00
SEE BELOW FOR OPTIONAL
BREAKFAST DEAL'S
EAT IN OR TAKE-AWAY
On Toast
Burgers

INTERIOR, RETAIL & EVENT DESIGN

BDP

16 Brewhouse Yard / Clerkenwell / London EC1V 4LJ
T +44 (0)20 7812 8000 / F +44 (0)20 7812 8399
simon.paddison@bdp.com
www.bdp.com

Management Martin Cook
Contact Simon Paddison
Staff 50 **Founded** 1972

Company Profile

BDP Design is a multi-discipline design group with a wide range of skills and expertise across both public and private sectors. Our experience spans retail, leisure, education, workplace, healthcare and transport design.

Our key strength lies in the integration of a wide range of creative services and solutions from a single source. Numerous leading brands are represented by many of our clients, with whom we have formed lasting relationships in both the UK and throughout Europe.

We believe in bringing the best skills and experience together to produce customer-focussed solutions.

1 Cardiff Library
2 Whiteleys Refurbishment, London
3 Westminster Academy
4 PricewaterhouseCoopers, London

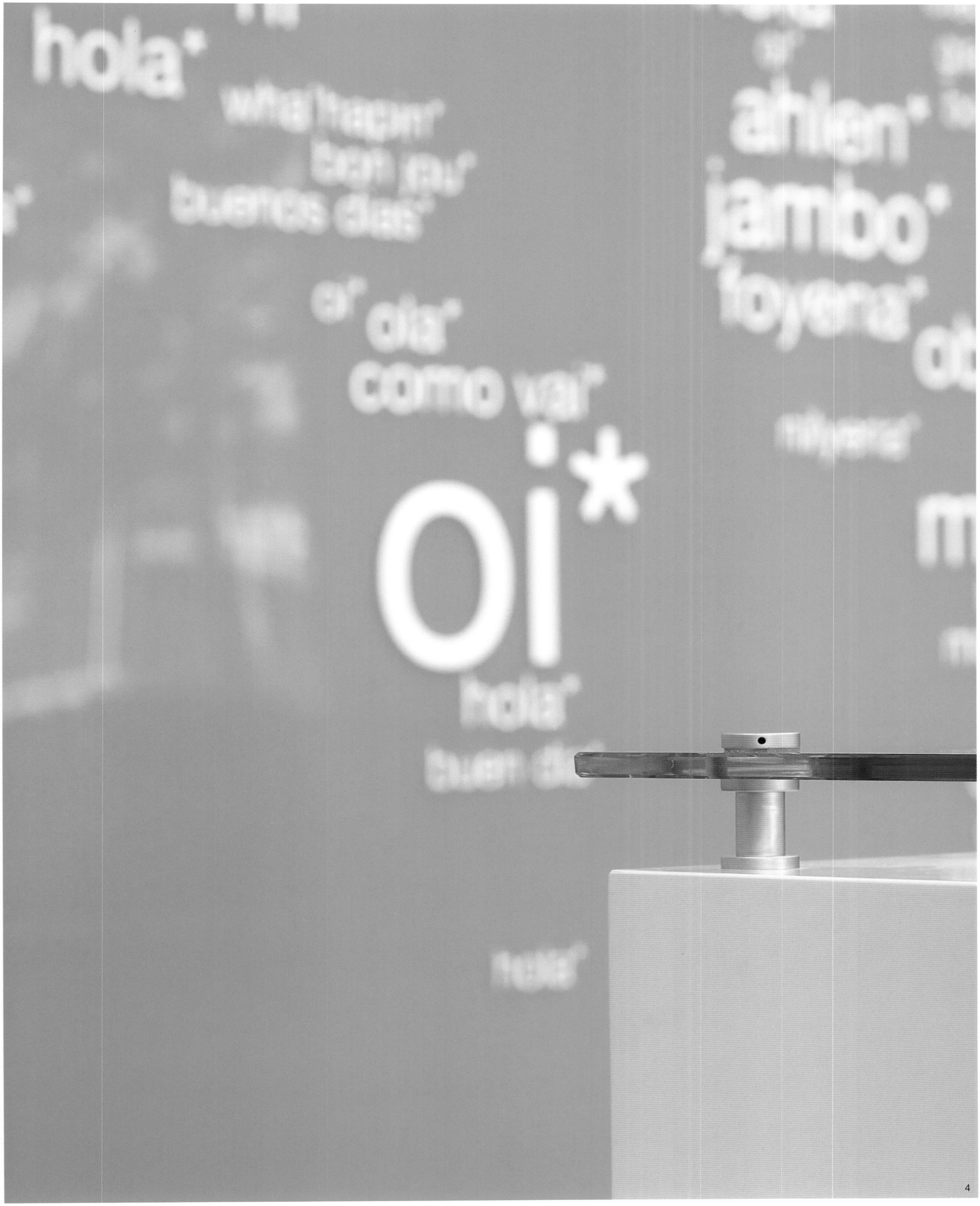

4

CampbellRigg

8 Apollo Studios / Charlton Kings Road /
London NW5 2SB
T +44 (0)20 7284 1515 / F +44 (0)20 7267 4112
design@campbellrigg.com
www.campbellrigg.com

Management Campbell Rigg, Dorota Czernuszewicz
Contact Dorota Czernuszewicz
Founded 1987

Company Profile
CampbellRigg has over 20 years of experience
providing strategic and creative design solutions
for some of the world's most successful companies.

An independent agency, we are renowned
for our international work in retail interiors and
communications across a broad range of markets
including food and non-food, textiles and banking.
The quality of our work has been recognised with
National and International awards from industry-
leading publications such as Retail Week and
Retail Interiors.

We believe in retail design excellence – using
imagination, intuition and financial common sense
to find the right solution. We can add real economic
value to your retail business using our extensive
experience in providing the following services:

– Strategy
– Brand Creation & Corporate Identity
– Graphic Communication
– Retail Interiors & Architecture
– Format Planning
– Merchandising
– Project Implementation

Our skilled multilingual team of strategic planners,
interior & graphic designers and architects have
worked with clients based across the globe including:

Austria: Interspar AG
Finland: Kesko OY
Germany: Adler GmbH (Metro), Kaufhof AG (Metro),
OBI GmbH (Tengelmann)
Ireland: Musgrave
Russia: Investproject, Victoria
Sweden: ICA OY, Hennes & Mauritz OY
Switzerland: Manor AG, Ukraine, Continium

United Kingdom: Asda (Wal-Mart), Argos, Arcadia,
Bacardi Global Retail, Blockbuster (UK) Ltd, Courtald
Textiles plc, Country Casuals, Comet Group plc,
Dixon Stores plc, Interbrew (UK) Ltd, Harrods
Ltd, Harvey Nichols plc, Marks and Spencer plc,
McDonalds Ltd, Safeway plc, Tesco plc, Unilever plc

Recent Awards
Retail Week 2009 Store Design of the Year (Finalist)
Retail Interiors 2006 Best In-Store
Communications (Winner)

See also Branding and Graphic Design p. 28

www.campbellrigg.com

bellrigg

retail design excellence

Argos Retail

Checkland Kindleysides

Charnwood Edge / Cossington / Leicester LE7 4UZ
T +44 (0)116 2644 700
info@checklandkindleysides.com
www.checklandkindleysides.com

Management Jeff Kindleysides, Founder;
Claire Callaway, Managing Director
Staff 80 **Founded** 1979

Agency Profile and Expertise
We are an independent design company, with a
unique culture that has developed and grown over
30 years. Our creativity is driven by robust customer,
design and market insight and an ability to make
things work aesthetically, physically and commercially.
We're collaborative by nature, we'll lead, steer and
inspire, but we'll also listen. It is this ability that has
created many long standing client relationships.

Clients
Asda
Boots
British Heart Foundation
BSM
Camelot
Clarks
Converse
Dockers
Hammersons
Henri Lloyd
Levi Strauss
Procter & Gamble
Royal Bank of Scotland
Ruby & Millie
Sony PlayStation
Superdrug
Timberland
Triumph
Vision Express
WGSN

Conferences
HiBrand 2008 – Moscow
In-Store Asia 2008 – Mumbai
In-Store Show 2008 – London
Retail Design Dynamics 2008 – London
EasyFairs, Shop Innovations 2008 – London

Awards
– ARE Design Awards 2009
  Timberland Westfield
– Chain Store Age Awards 2008
  Timberland Westfield – Store Exterior
– DBA Design Effectiveness Awards 2007
  Ruby & Millie – Gold – Interiors Retail & Leisure
– ISP/VM+SD 2007 International Store Design Award
  Sony Ericsson – Speciality Store
– Retail Interiors Awards 2007
  Sony Ericsson – General Merchandise Design
– POPAI UK Awards 2007
  Ruby & Millie – Gold – Cosmetics
  Ruby & Millie – Overall Winner – Display of the Year

1 Levi's Berlin Flagship Store
2 Converse 1HUND(RED) Exhibition
3 Timberland Westfield, London
4 George, Brand Identity
5 Sony PlayStation Grand Turismo 5 Prologue
   Driving Simulator Pod

1

2

3

George.

4

5

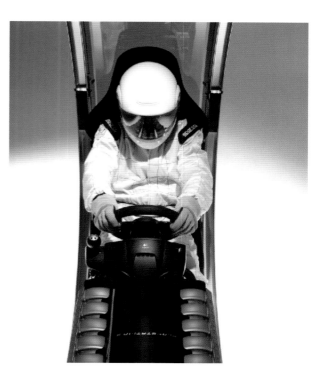

checkland kindleysides

Dalziel and Pow

5-8 Hardwick Street / London EC1R 4RG
T +44 (0)20 7837 7117
d.wright@dalziel-pow.co.uk
www.dalziel-pow.co.uk

Management David Dalziel, Creative Director;
Rosalyn Scott, Managing Director
Contact David Wright, Associate Director, Marketing
Staff 70 **Founded** 1983

Company Profile

A leading international creative agency, focused on design to connect our clients with their customers. We understand the requirement to maximise a return from any investment, and investment in design is often a key differentiator to success. We have many examples throughout our portfolio, where our work has delivered between 20% and 70% uplift in sales.

Our client coverage extends around the globe and we have built projects worldwide, from New York to Tokyo and São Paulo to Mumbai. This global exposure is a valuable creative tool, as we harness our experiences and build our understanding of diverse cultures and new trends.

Clients

Bank, Barratts, Canon (Europe), Cotton On (Global), Cross (Europe), Currys, Duffer (Japan), Gap (Europe), Globus (India), HMV, Hugo Boss, Illum (Denmark), JD, John Lewis, Jones, Lee (Global), Magasin (Denmark), Mom & Me – Mahindra Retail (India), Motivi (Italy), NBAD (Abu Dhabi), NCR (Global), Next, Nokia (Global), Plaisio (Greece), Primark (Europe), River Island (Europe), Sainsbury's, Save the Children, Store Twenty One, Tatuum (Europe), Tesco, TK Maxx, TM Lewin, Topshop (Global), Toyota (Global), Villandry, World Duty Free, Wrangler (Global)

Awards

Retail Week 2009
Store Design of the Year, Sainsbury's

Retail Interiors 2007
Best UK Retail Interior, Primark

Retail Interiors 2007
Fashion Retail Interior of the Year, Primark

Retail VM & Display 2007
Best In-store Branding, JD

Retail VM & Display 2007
Best Store Concept, River Island

Retail Interiors 2006
Best Out-of-Town Store, Blacks

Retail Week 2006
Store Design of the Year, River Island

Retail Interiors 2005
Best Small Shop, Speedo

Retail Interiors 2004
Fashion Retail Interior of the Year, River Island

DESIGN FOR BRANDS

DALZIEL + POW

THE VALUE OF DESIGN

Good design delivers strong financial performance. Retail branding and design are second only to product in convincing shoppers that one store is better than the competition. All successful brands employ design as part of their strategic development and this is true in all market sectors, from premium to value.

This year has seen our clients prosper and our services expand to fulfil the needs of today's marketplace. We are as busy as ever, responding to the ever-changing retail landscape with creative and effective Design for Brands.

JD
CURRYS
STORE TWENTY ONE

TOPSHOP
PRIMARK
CANON
NEXT

SAINSBURY'S
MOM & ME
NEXT

FOUR IV

11 Northburgh Street / London EC1V 0AN
T +44 (0)20 7336 1344 / F +44 (0)20 7336 1345
simont@fouriv.com
www.fouriv.com

Management Chris Dewar Dixon, Andy Bone,
Simon Thompson
Contact Simon Thompson
Staff 28 **Founded** 1989

Company Profile
FOUR IV is a leading UK based graphic and interior
design agency.

Specialising in brand development and retail & leisure
interior design, FOUR IV is the creative agency behind
some of the world's most exciting and commercially
proven luxury retail and leisure brands.

Currently working in over 14 countries, we are now in
our 20th year.

Clients
Browns
Burberry
Emporio Armani
Dunhill
Dinny Hall
Duchamp
Gas
Gieves and Hawkes
Hawkshead
Kurt Geiger
Liberty
Luella
Mulberry
Thomas Pink
Timberland
American Golf
Boots
DFS
Habitat
Mamas and Papas
Sothebys
Wedgwood
Harvey Nichols
Harrods
John Lewis Partnership
Arnotts
Unitim
Fenwick
Bouwfonds MAB
CBRE
Westfield
Abu Dhabi Tourism Authority
Athenæum
The Grove
InterContinental
Jumeirah Beach
Runnymede
The Langham
Nyonya
First Choice
Carlton Savannah Hotel
Utell

**See also Branding and Graphic Design p.48 and
New Media Design p.166**

NAKED, ISTANBUL

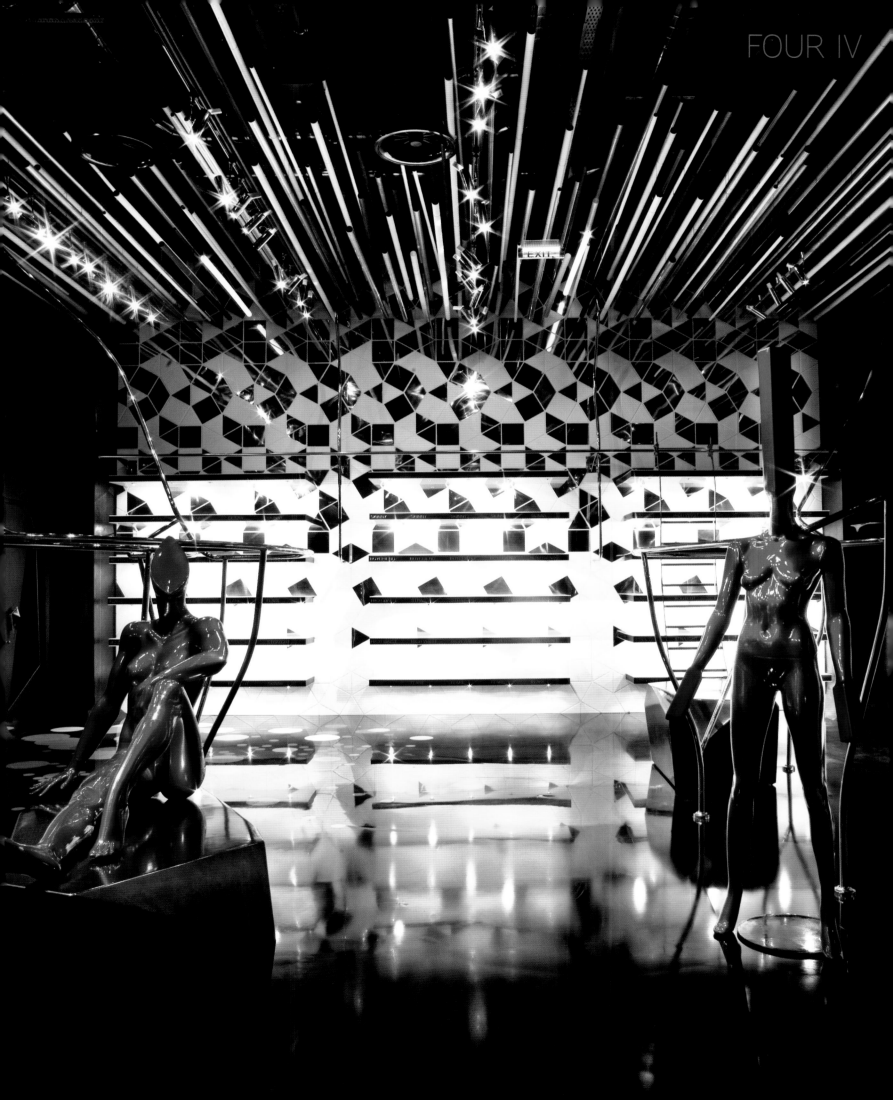

MAMAS AND PAPAS

FENWICK

HARVEY NICHOLS

HARVEY NICHOLS

DUCHAMP

HARRODS

THOMAS PINK

MULBERRY

Gensler

Aldgate House / 33 Aldgate High Street /
London EC3N 1AH
T +44 (0)207 073 9600
jon_tollit@gensler.com
www.gensler.com

Company Profile
Retail environments are the physical embodiment of a
client's brand. We believe our role as retail architects
is to create 'journeys' for customers—attracting them
to the store, engaging them with the products and
services, and extending the experience into their daily
lives. This journey is a pattern of interactions that give
customers a sense of connection with a brand.

Design Services
Prototype Store Development
Retail Architecture
Store Planning & Test Fits
Fixture Design
Trade Show Design
Brand Identity & Graphic Design
In-Store Brand Communications

Implementation Services
Design Guidelines
Prototype Standards
Construction Documentation
Construction Administration
Fabrication Coordination
Roll-Out Architectural Services
Roll-Out Process Development

Clients
Alghanim Electronics
Apple
Armani AX
Banana Republic
Chevrolet
Christian Dior
Dean & Deluca
Dockers
Gap
General Motors
Giorgio Armani
Haworth
McGregor
MS Retail
NatWest
Nike
Nissan
Royal Bank of Scotland
Starbucks
Suit Supply
World Retail Congress

See also Branding and Graphic Design p. 52

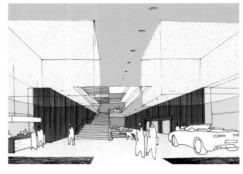

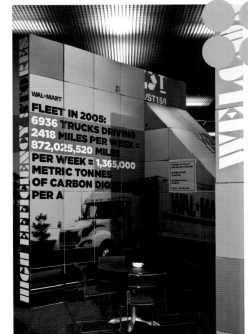

HUB DESIGN

Studio 414 The Big Peg / Vyse Street /
Birmingham B18 6NF
T +44 (0)121 685 8844
tony@hubdesignuk.com

Exhibition Stands
Interiors
New Media
Events
Shopfits
Specialist Projects

1   Perkins Interior - Peterborough
2   Perkins Interior - Peterborough
3   Henleys - Bull Ring Birmingham
4   Low Carbon House - Trafalgar Square
5   Low Carbon House - Trafalgar Square
6   Caterpillar Stand - Las Vegas

Invisiblecities

Ostlers cottage / Watergate / Locksash Lane /
West Marden PO18 9EQ
T +44 (0)2392 631 221 / T +44 (0)7762 067 833
adam@invisiblecities.co.uk
www.invisiblecities.co.uk

Contact Adam Howard
Staff 4 **Founded** 2000

Company Profile
We provide clients with realistic 3d images and
animations of their concepts. We work for interior
designers, product designers, marketing companies,
book publishers and broadcast TV.

Clients
WATG
GA Design
Alex Kravetz Design
Swanke Hayden Connell
David Collins Studio
Nokia
Gallaher
Digit
Dorling Kindersley
Richmond international

1 Private house Tergedine associates
2 Trianon Hotel Restaurant. Richmond International
3 Soho Sanctum Hotel. Candocan
4 Chateau St Tropez. Steven Taylor Associates
5 Chateau St Tropez. Steven Taylor Associates

1

2

3

4

5

NewEdge + The Brewery
End to end innovation

18 Petersham Road / Richmond / London TW10 6UW
T +44 (0)20 8439 8400 / F +44 (0)20 8439 8410
london@newedge-thebrewery.com
www.newedge-thebrewery.com

Management Paul Stead, Co CEO
Pam Henderson Ph.D., Co CEO
Contact Paul Stead
Staff 50

Company Profile
NewEdge + The Brewery brings you a new type
of consultancy.

Award-winning design combines with business
strategy and disruptive research to deliver powerful
new approaches to growth through brand, packaging,
product and environmental solutions.

We've worked with many of the world's largest
brands through to some of the smallest start ups.
In every case we challenge you to think differently,
disrupt the norm and uncover attractive opportunities.

Call us for a strategic approach to design and
innovation that delivers outstanding business results.

Left Brain + Right Brain
Logic + Creativity
Growth + Innovation
NewEdge + The Brewery

Clients
Air Products
Boeing
Colgate-Palmolive
DSM
DuPont
Eastman
Ferrari
John Deere
Kellogg
Microsoft
Molson Coors
Motorola
Procter & Gamble
Solae
Waterstone's
Weyerhauser

**See also Branding and Graphic Design p. 80 and
Packaging Design p. 136**

Creating opportunities in every space

Adding value to the customer experience through
engaging store landscaping, inspiring communications
and creating a compelling brand experience.

REINVIGORATE Ltd
Retail Design & Build

Kestrel Court / Harbour Rd. / Portishead /
Bristol BS20 7AN
T +44 (0)800 500 7090 / F +44 (0)800 500 7091
martin@reinvigorate.co.uk
www.reinvigorate.co.uk

Management Founder & 2 Board Directors
Staff 12 **Founded** 2003
Contact Martin Monks

Company Profile
Reinvigorate is a Brand Design and Project
Management agency. We can provide a complete
'Turn Key' solution; from Brand positioning and
communication through to delivery and installation
of a Brand's in-store experience. Reinvigorate can
deliver a total brand experience from the creation
and conception of the brand through to the full
brand experience in store.

We have the capabilities and expertise to deliver
profitable business solutions for any brand in any
format from stand alone or a concession; through
to single free standing units in a third party store.
In addition to designing the brand experience we
also Project Manage the installation and construction
of the full retail environment within the client's
specified budget.

Clients
Adams Childrenswear
Brooks Brothers
Brantano
Ermes
Hallmark Cards
Jacques Vert
Jawad Business Group
Moda in Pelle
Pixi Beauty
Planet
Things Accessories
Terra Plana

See also Branding and Graphic Design p.94

1 TERRA PLANA
   Flagship Store - London, UK
2 THINGS ACCESSORIES
   Flagship store – Slovakia, Bratislava
3 BRANTANO SHOE CITY
   New concept store - Dubai, U.A.E.
4 PEARSONS DEPARTMENT STORE
   New concept store - London, UK
5 PLANET
   New concept store - London, UK
6 ADAMS KIDS
   New concept store – Abu Dhabi, U.A.E.
7 ADAMS KIDS
   Flagship store – St. Petersburg, Russia
8 PIXI BEAUTICIANS
   New concept store – Dubai, U.A.E.

1

2

3

4

5

5

7

8

REINVIGORATE

RETAIL DESIGN AND BUILD

Sedley Place Ltd.
www.sedley-place.co.uk

68 Venn Street / London SW4 0AX
T +44 (0)207 627 5777 / F+44 (0)207 627 5859
info@sedley-place.co.uk
www.sedley-place.co.uk

Management Mick Nash
Contacts Antonio Maduro, Alastair Patrick
Staff 30 **Founded** 1978

Company Profile
Sedley Place is an independent design agency.
Our skills are diverse: from brand strategies to graphic
design, product design to premium packaging, interior
and architectural design to digital media.

We have offices in London and Edinburgh and we
work with businesses and organisations of all sizes
all over the world.

At Sedley Place, you'll find empathy and intelligence.
We offer a potent mix of traditional craftsmanship
and leading technology, art and design, precision
detailing and grand scale vision. We pride ourselves
on our ability to provide original creative solutions that
surprise and delight.

Simply put, we build desire.

Interior and architectural design
For us, spaces are an important extension of the
people and the brands that inhabit them. They are
not merely functional; they also communicate an
important message through the user experience.

- Work places
- Hotels and resorts
- Restaurants and bars
- Private houses

Our unique combination of craft skill and imagination
combine to create interiors and buildings that are
diverse in style; from sumptuous to minimalist,
calming to stimulating, traditional to cutting edge.
Our aim is to couple the desire to be truly original
with a deep understanding of our clients' needs in
order to create outstanding environments for life,
work and leisure.

Clients
Jumeirah Golf Estates
TBWA Advertising
Savills
Cumbria Tourism
The Gleneagles Hotel
Buddha Bar

**See also Branding and Graphic Design p. 96,
Packaging Design p. 146 and New Media
Design p. 174**

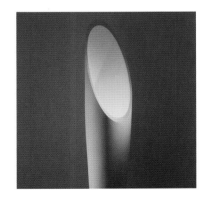

Shopkit Group Limited

Units B & C / 100 Cecil Street / Watford /
Hertfordshire WD24 5AD
T +44 (0)1923 818282 / F +44 (0)1923 818280
sales@shopkit.com
www.shopkit.com

Management David Turner, David Hunt
Contact Paul McCarthy
Staff 23 **Founded** 1980

Company Profile
Shopkit Group of companies are experienced in all
types of interiors, including shops, offices, banks,
restaurants, window displays and exhibitions, offering
clients a complete design and build service, from the
initial concept/planning stages, through manufacture
and on to complete installation.
Included in the products and services provided by
Shopkit is the most comprehensive range of display
equipment, low-voltage lighting, cabinets, partition
systems and cable and rod suspension systems
available today.
Continuing to expand worldwide Shopkit has offices
and showrooms in Germany, Spain, Portugal, Dubai,
USA and Canada.
Shopkit manufactures all their own product in a
purpose built factory in the UK.

Clients
Arthur Anderson Consulting, Apple, BBC, BMW a.G.,
BP Plc, British Airways Travel Shops, British Telecom,
GSK Glaxo Smith Kline, Harrods, Hasbro,
HDI Versicherung AG., Hitachi Data Systems Limited,
IBM UK Limited, The London Stock Exchange,
Lotus Cars, G.E. Money, JP Morgan Chase Bank,
Nortel Networks plc, Portugal Telecom,
Renault UK Limited, Charles Schwab Europe,
Selfridges & Co, Shell UK Exploration, Sony,
Sparkasse, Westfield Ltd

1, 9   TracKit – a versatile track suspension
        system, giving mobility and flexibility to the
        presentation of graphics, sliding panels,
        shelving and clothing displays, available
        in single or multi-track versions with many
        accessories
2   Cabinets – a comprehensive range of sizes,
        colours and materials, available in standard
        sizes or custom made
3   Low-Level Screening – a modular system that
        can be configured to suit individual planning
        requirements. Panel widths, heights and
        materials to specification, with a variety of
        shelving options available
4, 6, 8 Mast System – a unique patented concept
        in tensioned cables, using the strength
        and simplicity of a rigid mast as a versatile
        support for a virtually limitless range of
        accessories. Units can be free standing, wall
        to floor or ceiling to floor fixed and can easily
        incorporate a variety of panels to create
        screening in different heights, as well as low-
        voltage lighting
5, 7   Bespoke backlit acrylic wall with shelving,
        illuminated display cubes and other display
        systems created for Patrick Cox UK flagship
        store, London

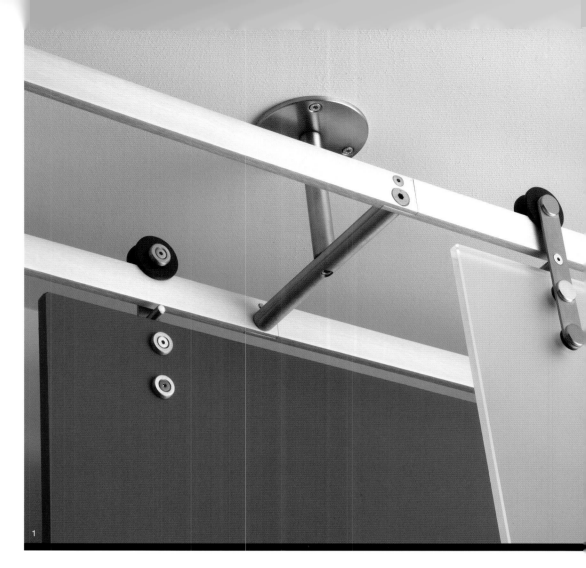

1

2

3

Philip Watts Design

Unit 11: Byron Industrial Estate / Brookfield Road /
Arnold / Nottingham NG5 7ER
T +44 (0)115 926 9756 / F +44 (0)115 920 5395
sales@philipwattsdesign.com
www.philipwattsdesign.com

Management Philip Watts
Contact Philip Watts
Staff 10 **Founded** 1994

Company Profile
Formed from modest roots in 1994, Philip Watts
Design has continually grown both in size and
creativity.
Our highly successful creative architectural
ironmongery range, spearheaded by the innovative
portholes for doors kits has helped form a family
of over 120 products, regularly specified for both
national and international projects.
This design and build mentality has helped to push
the interior side of the business forwards with
increasingly challenging projects and installations.
Our strengths rest in developing full concepts from
name generation through to opening the night. We
work closely with our clients and are flexible enough
to accept un-forseen deviations and changes to
original specifications.
The Philip Watts Design style is usually signified by a
subtle blend of creativity, experience and irreverence.
This can be found in any of our projects from melting
aluminium staircases to Tokyo-chic restaurants.

Clients
Interiors:
YO! Sushi
Le Bistrot Pierre
Ego Restaurants
Elevate UK Ltd

Products:
BBC
Virgin
Channel 4
LWT
Heathrow Airport
Burger King
McDonalds
Costa Coffee
Conran
Gillette
Elton John
Nicholas Grimshaw Architects
Kodak
BMW

Awards
FX Magazine Interior Design Practice of the year 2007
FX Magazine Best Leisure product winner 2004
FX Magazine Commercial fixture or fitting finalist 2007

Nottingham Creative Business Awards; Architecture,
Interior Design and Urban, winner 2007
Nottingham Creative Business Awards; Architecture,
Interior Design and Urban, finalist 2008

Adex Design for Excellence, gold winner 2005
Adex Design for Excellance, platinum winner 2006

1-2   Yo! Sushi, Nottingham
3-6   Yo! Sushi, Brunswick, London
7   Yo! Sushi, Liverpool
8   Yo! Sushi, Spinningfields
10-12   Ego, Prestwich
13-16   Le Bistrot Pierre, Sheffield
17-18   PWD Ironmongery products
19   Sculptural staircase, Northampton
20-22   Kingly Club, St. Martins Lane, London

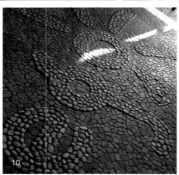

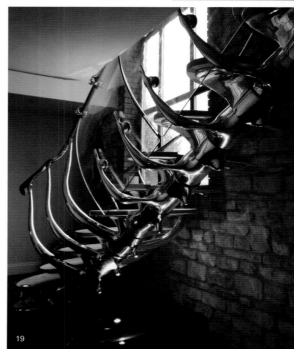

7

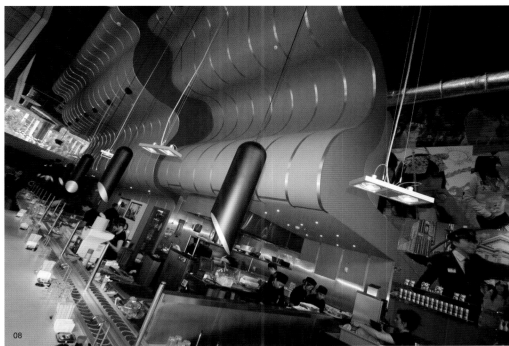

08

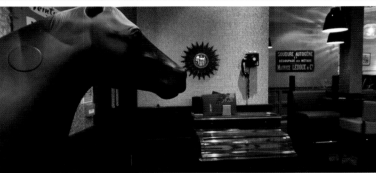

3

4

15

16

0

21

22

James Williamson Design Ltd
Product & Interior Design Consultant

Unit 18 – New Crescent Yard / Acton Lane /
London NW10 8SJ
T +44 (0)208 965 0804
james@jameswilliamson.com
www.jameswilliamson.com

Founded 2007

Company Profile

James Williamson is a designer with over 15 years experience in the design industry with a successful CV of products and interior spaces.

A student of Central Saint Martins Art College and 6 years of design and engineering studies are the foundation of his success.

His work ensures a perfect blend of aesthetics, form and function, with great emphasis for attention to detail.

Mission

The creations of James Williamson always try to place a smile on one's face by applying emotions, memories and humour in a contemporary manner.

Every product and space require a story with a poetic meaning and is achieved through methodical study of a given topic.

Services

Product & furniture design
Concept generation and evaluation
2D detailed manufacturing drawings
3D solid modelling – parts and assemblies

Interior design
Concept schemes and mood boards
2D layout plans and elevation drawings
FF&E specification cost schedules
3D schematics and visualisation

Project Management
Product design – concept to manufacture
Interior design – bars, restaurants, spa's and residential property.

Clients

Interior and furniture design
Mews of Mayfair – www.mewsofmayfair.com
Marco Pierre White – www.theyewtree.net
Elemis Day Spa – Mayfair – www.elemis.com
Farm Club – Switzerland – Concept luxury WC's
Chelsea Arts College – New Café concepts
Residential property in North London

Product design
Lisa Tse Ltd – Air revitaliser unit
Chivas Regal – Promotional display cabinet
Product Solutions – Mobile access tower system
SGB Youngman – Access equipment
Homebase – Plastic multi functional tool tray's
GSK – Oral hygiene concepts
Maxon Communications – Cordless telephone concepts

knock-knock®

TAKE AWAY

1.45 p	1.95 p	Chilli Con Carne with Chips	3.30 p
	2.25 p	Savoury Mince with Chips	3.30 p
2.40 p	2.55 p	Cheese & Chips	2.25 p
	2.85 p	Beefburger Rolls	1.40 p
	245 p	Cheeseburgers	1.55 p
	1.70 p	1/4 Pound Beefburger	1.65 p
	1.30 p	1/4 Pound Cheeseburger	1.90 p
m Pie 1.70 p		1/4 Pound Burger	1.30 p
	1.25 p	Beefburger	80 p
70 p	1.20 p	Pea fritter	70 p
	75 p	Pineapple Fritters (2)	1.10 p
	80 p	Spicey Wedges	1.50 p
80 p	1.10 p	Spicey Spiral Fries	1.50 p
80 p	1.10 p	Sauce	10 p
80 p	1.10 p	Bread & Butter	30 p
5 p	75 p	Pickled Onions	15 p
	1.00 p	Pickled Eggs	45 p
	1.35 p	Cockles	1.90 p
(7)	1.60 p	Eggburger	1.70 p
		Chicken in a Bun	2.15 p
	1.85 p	Onion Rings (7)	1.05 p
		Coleslaw	80 p
Peas,		Sandwiches to Order From	1.75
		Chip Butty	1.25 p
	2.65 p	Turkey Stick	
	2.75 p	Pancake Rolls	1.00 p
	2.95 p		
	2.90 p		
	3.30 p		
	3.30 p		
	3.30 p		
	1.45 p		

Cheese Burger with Bacon

Small £2.25

Large £2.60

Jackets

ON ARE VE

To suit the occasion

ASK FOR ...the original Lincolnshire Fish Cake

£ 75p

King Frost

Do yourself - they're Britain's favou

DAL for good

Cooked Chicken Portions

Chicken 'n' Chips

£3.90

Delicious DEEP ROUND Qualipies

£1.70

Available in 4 TRADITIONAL fillings

ONION THE ALL ROUND

£1.05p

Chick Steal IN GOLDEN CRISPY BA

£2.15

NOT WITH CH

FISH KED DER

BIG MOUTH BILLY BASS

A

45p

ADVERTS

Sign Design Society

There are few things in life that affect everyone, which we've all experienced and on which most of us have a view. Signing is one of them.

Sign Design Society talks & events:

The Society's very regular programme of activities is centred around talks held at various London locations and given by leading speakers from around the world.

The subject matter is both rich and varied, stimulating much discussion. In the last year for example this has ranged from the story of the new St Pancras Station, through how the UK National Border is being consistently signed for the first time, to why the design of the London Underground map is due for serious review. We've also heard about advances in personal navigation through GPS and how technology is making life easier for those involved in highways sign design and planning.

Ranging further afield, we learned how a new bus information system caused something of a social revolution in Santiago, Chile and how new discipline with shop signs and advertising is improving the environment in the ancient city of Amman in Jordan, a challenge very different from that faced by modern Dubai, covered in an earlier talk.

In 2008, just before it opened, the Terminal 5 design team talked to us about the wayfinding solution for this great modern building and a year later a visit to site allowed members to see how a highly complex system was working in practice. More recently a guided tour of pedestrian signing initiatives in London gave an insight into the politics of communicating the capital to visitors.

Our most prestigious event - The Sign Design Awards - is held regularly and, whilst the 2009 competition is now closed, an exhibition of the entries is to be held in London and Vienna later in the year. For full details of all talks and events, please visit the website.

But whilst good signing is often unnoticed, bad signing is always frustrating and can be dangerous and life-threatening.

The Sign Design Society's purpose is to promote greater awareness in the design disciplines, industry, education and government of the importance played by good signing and wayfinding in making our increasingly complex public environments easier to understand and more comfortable and safer to use.

We draw together people active in all areas of signing - communication and graphic design, architecture, manufacture and client - at regular meetings for talks by invited speakers on an eclectic range of subjects.

The Society also publishes the Sign Design Guide, a primary industry tool, jointly with the RNIB and regularly runs the international Sign Design Awards competition, to reward excellence and encourage new ideas.

Membership brings many benefits:
- regular meetings with talks from guest speakers and lively discussion, free of charge
- visits to places of interest, involvement in seminars, conferences etc.
- links across the world with like-minded organisations and people
- contacts and news over all areas of the industry
- in-house journal 'Directions'
- communication between members via the website
- help to educational establishments
- contributions to publications
- influence in the fields of standardisation and legislation
- problem-solving advice and help from fellow members.

Take a look at our website **www.signdesignsociety.co.uk** or contact our Administrator, Michelle Henderson-Vieira.

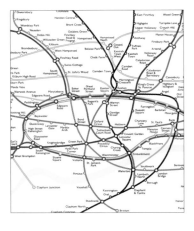

The Sign Design Society, 5 Longton Grove, Sydenham, London SE26 6QQ
t. +44 (0)20 8776 8866 f. +44 (0)871 900 3160
e. enquiries@signdesignsociety.co.uk w. www.signdesignsociety.co.uk

Subscribe and get ____

+ FRAME **sealed and delivered** TO YOUR DOORSTEP
+ UP TO **35% discount** ON THE RETAIL PRICE
+ A **cool gift**
+ **10% discount** ON ALL FRAME BOOKS
+ **50% discount** ON A 1-YEAR SUBSCRIPTION TO FRAME DIGITAL

rule
07

Style
is
not to be
Trusted

Ridiculous Design Rules, Ridiculous Advertising Rules
and Ridiculous Fashion Rules

In bookstores now

BISPUBLISHERS
www.bispublishers.nl

ELEPHANT

THE ART & VISUAL CULTURE MAGAZINE

ISSUE №1

SÃO PAULO GUIDE

PETER SAVILLE

COLLAGE   BIKES & FASHION

FERNANDO GUTIÉRREZ

ART & THE INTERNET

NEW TRENDS

STUDIO VISITS   UNIT PUBLISHING

AUTUMN 2009

ELEPHANT MAGAZINE
The Art & Visual Culture Magazine

The past 20 years have seen an increasing polarization of the visual arts with, on the one hand, the art world proper and, on the other, what has so far been known as applied arts, or commercial art. Meanwhile, the most interesting work seems to have been happening in the middle. Fashion designers thinking like artists, artists thinking like fashion designers, artists who are not afraid of engaging with new technologies, digital artists who are not afraid of engaging with art history, painters working with graphic devices, graphic designers working with concepts, sculptors whose work looks like design, designers whose work looks like sculpture... Not to mention all the art forms that fall directly into the gap: illustration, graffiti art, screen-printing, etc. Are they art, or commercial art? And who cares? It is this vast and vital space in the middle, with its vibrant culture and endlessly changing 'scene', that is the subject

SH DESIGN 2011/12

...ion of this survey of leading British design agencies and studios is
...r publication in the autumn of 2011. It will provide the most
...ve profile of design in the UK, offering clients both in the UK
...an essential guide to design services in the UK.

...tfolio on the
...'s desk!

...mpaign covering the UK and the Benelux
...usive pre-subscription discount. It targets
...yers and professionals in marketing,
...blic relations.

...design buyers within a broad range
...nercial and cultural sectors will receive
...copy of the volume.

Be part of it and don't let
your name be left out!

If you are a designer or design agency located in the
are interested in being included with a showcase pro
next edition, please contact us.

Contact

Contact our sales manager Marijke Wervers at BIS P
for information on how to submit your work, closure
and conditions.

Marijke Wervers can be best reached at marijke@bisp
Tel: +31(0)20- 515 0230

2011/12

British Design has a specific focus – highlighting the top talent in the UK for a primarily continental audience. That fits our offer perfectly."

Steve Osborne – Managing Director,
Osborne Pike Ltd

British Design is a stylish and comprehensive sourcebook showcasing the best in contemporary design; it is a must-have for all design professionals and those commissioning high quality design services."

Stephen Anderson – Design Director, BDP

"We advertise in only a few design directories, but *British Design* is one in which we like to be included every time. The work is displayed beautifully with a clear layout, allowing us to present our latest projects."

Abigail Lloyd-Jones – PR Manager,
Checkland Kindleysides

"We have advertised in the *British Design* book since it began. It is always high quality, exuding gravitas and a fresh design approach – a useful tool for attracting new clients."

Salvatore Cicero – Managing Director,
Two by Two Design

"The *British Design* book is an invaluable reference point for all that is positive in British design and a great platform for British design on the global stage."

David Wright – Associate Director -Marketing,
Dalziel & Pow Design Consultants

"We all agree *British Design* is amongst the best in the world and gives PureEquator the chance to showcase its work to a diverse audience. It is a well-thought-out publication, with emphasis on the actual projects, giving its readers a living portfolio of talent."

David Rogers – Global Creative Director,
PureEquator

"The *British Design* book is the only directory that truly believes in showcasing the breadth of British creative talent; therefore, we are proud to accompany some fine companies in its pages."

Olly Guise – Design Director, Taxi Studio

"A great showcase of the best in British design and an invaluable reference."

Lance Bates – Manager Marketing Operations,
Toyota (GB) PLC

"A beautifully presented book, a valuable addition to our library and will assist us to make contact with relevant design agencies when required."

Katie Preston – Retail Design Manager,
Westfield London

"The *British Design* publication is very useful and a good way to spot new designers and talent."

Sarah Rowen – Best Practice Manager,
Atos Origin

"This is a welcome addition to my desktop. It will be very useful, very inspiring and I will use it should we find ourselves looking for a brand agency."

Kate Cowan – Head of Marketing and PR,
Hay Group

"As a tea company with a mainstream, multiple-stocked brand, we find this publication very useful. Beautiful presentation and comprehensive design company coverage make this a very desirable reference book."

Ross Thompson - Director, Punjana Tea

PARTICIPATING AGENCIES BY LOCATION

ADDRESSES

Accept & Proceed
Studio 2 / Peachy Edwards House /
1 Teesdale Street / London E2 6GF
T +44 (0)20 7199 1030
info@acceptandproceed.com
www.acceptandproceed.com

The Adhere Creative
Studio 34 / Fazeley Studios / 191 Fazeley Street /
Birmingham B55SE
T +44 (0)121 2850529
info@theadherecreative.com
www.theadherecreative.com

Anywhichway
81 Rivington Street / London EC2A 3AY
T +44 (0)20 3178 6380
hello@anywhichway.co.uk
www.anywhichway.co.uk

Bark Design Limited
Studio 5 / Panther House 38 / Mount Pleasant /
London WC1X 0AP
T +44 (0)207 8373116 / F +44 (0)207 8373116
bark@barkdesign.net
www.barkdesign.net

BDP
16 Brewhouse Yard / Clerkenwell /
London EC1V 4LJ
T +44 (0)20 7812 8000 / F +44 (0)20 7812 8399
simon.paddison@bdp.com
www.bdp.com

Beef
Unit 4.3 Paintworks / Bristol BS4 3EH
T +44 (0)117 971 1150
hello@wearebeef.co.uk
www.wearebeef.co.uk

The Brand Union
11-33 St John Street / London EC1M 4AA
T +44 (0)20 7559 7000 / F +44 (0)20 7559 7001
info@thebrandunion.com
www.thebrandunion.com

Build
Studio 112 / Hilton Grove /
12–15 Hatherley Mews / London E17 4QP
T +44 (0)208 5211040
informyou@wearebuild.com
www.wearebuild.com

Bulletproof
28-32 Shelton Street / Covent Garden /
London WC2H 9JE
T +44 (0)207 395 3636 / F +44 (0)207 395 3737
debbie@wearebulletproof.com
www.wearebulletproof.com

CampbellRigg
8 Apollo Studios / Charlton Kings Road /
London NW5 2SB
T +44 (0)20 7284 1515
F +44 (0)20 7267 4112
design@campbellrigg.com
www.campbellrigg.com

Chaos
Head Office:
32 High Street / Guildford / Surrey GU1 3EL
Offices: Guildford, London and Lausanne
T +44 (0)1483 557800 / F +44 (0)1483 537755
peter.c@chaosdesign.com
www.chaosdesign.com

Checkland Kindleysides
Charnwood Edge / Cossington /
Leicester LE7 4UZ
T +44 (0)116 2644 700
info@checklandkindleysides.com
www.checklandkindleysides.com

Crumpled Dog
18 Phipp Street / London EC2A 4NU
T +44 (0)20 7739 5553
christian@crumpled-dog.com
www.crumpled-dog.com

CURIOUS
19a Floral Street / London WC2E 9DS
T +44 (0)20 7240 6214
claire@curiouslondon.com
www.curiouslondon.com

D.Vision Create
48 Fitzroy Street / London W1T 5BS
T +44 (0)20 7681 0001
contact@dvisioncreate.com
www.dvisioncreate.com

Dalziel and Pow
5-8 Hardwick Street / London EC1R 4RG
T +44 (0)20 7837 7117
d.wright@dalziel-pow.co.uk
www.dalziel-pow.co.uk

Design Activity
Beech House / 6 St Pauls Road / Clifton /
Bristol BS8 1LT
T +44 (0)117 933 9400 / F +44 (0)117 923 9989
andrew.stroud@design-activity.co.uk
www.design-activity.co.uk

Design Project
Second Floor / 80A York Street / Leeds LS9 8AA
T +44 (0)113 234 1222
james@designproject.co.uk
www.designproject.co.uk

Designhouse
T +44 (0)20 8439 9360 / F +44 (0)20 8439 9373
74 Great Suffolk Street / London SE1 0BL
dh@designhouse.co.uk
www.designhouse.co.uk

Deviate
BBIC Innovation Way / Barnsley S75 1JL
T +44 (0)1226 720 072
James@WeAreDeviate.co.uk
www.WeAreDeviate.co.uk

Element 5.0
14 Blandford Square /
Newcastle upon Tyne NE1 4HZ
T +44 (0)191 255 4420 / F +44 (0)191 255 4421
info@element5design.com
www.element5design.com

Felton Communication
2 Bleeding Heart Yard / London EC1N 8SJ
T +44 (0)20 7405 0900 / F +44 (0)20 7430 1550
design@felton.co.uk
www.feltonworks.com

FL@33
59 Britton Street / London EC1M 5UU
T +44 (0)20 7168 7990
contact@flat33.com
flat33.com
stereohype.com
bzzzpeek.com
postcard-book.info
madeandsold.com

FOUR IV
11 Northburgh Street / London EC1V 0AN
T +44 (0)20 7336 1344 / F +44 (0)20 7336 1345
simont@fouriv.com
www.fouriv.com

Gensler
Aldgate House / 33 Aldgate High Street /
London EC3N 1AH
T +44 (0)207 073 9600
duncan_mackay@gensler.com
www.gensler.com

Greenwich Design
David Mews / 11a Greenwich South Street /
Greenwich / London SE10 8NJ
T +44 (0)20 8853 3028 / F +44 (0)20 8858 2128
hello@greenwich-design.co.uk
www.greenwich-design.co.uk

Tom Hingston Studio
76 Brewer Street / London W1F 9TX
T +44 (0)20 7287 6044 / F +44 (0)20 7287 6048
info@hingston.net
www.hingston.net

Holmes Wood
Studio 27 / 38 Burns Road / London SW11 5GY
T +44 (0)20 7326 9970 / F +44 (0)20 7350 2450
info@holmes-wood.com
www.holmes-wood.com

HUB DESIGN
Studio 414 The Big Peg / Vyse Street /
Birmingham B18 6NF
T +44 (0)121 685 8844
tony@hubdesignuk.com

Invisiblecities
Ostlers cottage / Watergate / Locksash Lane /
West Marden PO18 9EQ
T +44 (0)2392 631 221 / T +44 (0)7762 067 833
adam@invisiblecities.co.uk
www.invisiblecities.co.uk

Jake
Design Studio / Top Floor / 16 Bromley Road /
Kent BR3 5JE
T +44 (0)208 633 3962
hello@jake.uk.com
www.jake.uk.com

jones knowles ritchie
128 Albert Street / London NW1 7NE
T +44 (0)20 7428 8000 / F +44 (0)20 7428 8080
info@jkr.co.uk
www.jkr.co.uk

Kinneir Dufort
5 Host Street / Bristol BS1 5BU
T +44 (0)117 901 4000 / F +44 (0)117 901 4001
susanna.clasby@kinneirdufort.com
www.kinneirdufort.com

Kiosk
The Site Gallery / Brown Street /
Sheffield S1 2BS
T +44 (0)208 144 5908 (Skype™)
david@letskiosk.com
www.letskiosk.com

LAW Creative
LAW Creative – London
Ninety Long Acre / Covent Garden / London
WC2E 9RZ
T +44 (0)20 7849 3035

LAW Creative – Harpenden
Four Waterside / Station Road / Harpenden
Hertfordshire AL5 4US
T +44 (0)1582 469300 / F +44 (0)1582 460050
brett.sammels@lawcreative.co.uk
www.lawcreative.co.uk

Lisa Tse Ltd
Gresham House / 24 Holborn Viaduct /
London EC1A 2BN
T +44 (0)207 2489 248 / F +44 (0)207 9909 248
design@lisatse.com
www.lisatse.com

LPK
93-95 Gloucester Place / Suite G3 /
London W1U 6JQ
T +44 (0)20 7487 8251 / F +44 (0)20 7487 8477
cathy_lowe@lpk.com
www.lpk.com

Magpie Studio
2 The Hangar / Perseverance Works /
38 Kingsland Road / London E2 8DD
T +44 (0)20 7729 3007
hello@magpie-studio.com
www.magpie-studio.com

Make
504B The Big Peg / 120 Vyse Street /
Birmingham B18 6NF
T +44 (0)845 456 9592
studio@wearemake.com
www.wearemake.com

Multistorey
Studio 10 / 51 Derbyshire Street /
London E2 6JQ
T +44 (0)20 7729 8090
us@multistorey.net
www.multistorey.net

N1 Creative Ltd
Unit 3 / 11-29 Fashion Street / London E1 6PX
T +44 (0)20 7655 4321 / F +44 (0)20 7655 4575
info@n1creative.com
www.n1creative.com

NewEdge + The Brewery
18 Petersham Road / Richmond /
London TW10 6UW
T +44 (0)20 8439 8400 / F +44 (0)20 8439 8410
london@newedge-thebrewery.com
www.newedge-thebrewery.com

ADDRESSES

Objective
Objective Studio / The Courtyard /
17 West Street / Farnham / Surrey GU9 7DR
T +44 (0)1252 718 400 / F +44 (0)7092 844 589
hello@objectivestudio.com
www.objectivestudio.com

ODD
12-14 Berry Street / London EC1V 0AU
T +44 (0)20 7490 7900 / F +44 (0)20 7681 1688
info@thankodd.com
www.thankodd.com

One Black Bear
The Old School House / 191 Fazeley Street /
Birmingham B5 5SE
T +44(0)121 224 7963
info@oneblackbear.com
www.oneblackbear.com

ORB Creative
Studio 209b / The Big Peg / 120 Vyse Street /
Birmingham B18 6NF
T +44 (0)870 220 2648
info@orbcreative.com
www.orbcreative.com

Osborne Pike
22 Circus Mews / Bath BA1 2PW
T +44 (0)1225 489269 / F +44 (0)1225 469633
brandstories@osbornepike.co.uk
www.osbornepike.co.uk

Pancentric Digital
4-8 Emerson Street / Bankside / London SE1 9DU
T +44 (0)20 7099 6370
team@pancentric.com
www.pancentric.com

Parent
5 Park Place / North Road / Poole /
Dorset BH14 0LY
T +44(0)1202 717 333
mail@parentdesign.co.uk
www.parentdesign.co.uk

Pencil
Unit 8 / Westfield Court / Third Avenue /
Westfield Ind Est / Midsomer Norton /
Somerset BA3 4XD
T +44 (0)845 290 3930
info@penciluk.co.uk
www.penciluk.co.uk

Pixel DNA
Pixel DNA Limited / 32 Wellcarr Road /
Sheffield S8 8QQ
T +44 (0)114 220 2337
info@pixel-dna.com
www.pixel-dna.com

Pure Equator
The Old School House / The Heritage Centre /
High Pavement / The Lace Market /
Nottingham NG1 1HN
T +44 (0)115 9476 444/555 /
F +44 (0)115 9504 948
david.rogers@pure-equator.com
www.pure-equator.com

REINVIGORATE Ltd
Kestrel Court / Harbour Rd. / Portishead /
Bristol BS20 7AN
T +44 (0)800 500 7090 / F +44 (0)800 500 7091
martin@reinvigorate.co.uk
www.reinvigorate.co.uk

Sedley Place Ltd.
68 Venn Street / London SW4 0AX
T +44 (0)207 627 5777 / F +44 (0)207 627 5859
info@sedley-place.co.uk
www.sedley-place.co.uk

Shopkit Group Limited
Units B & C / 100 Cecil Street / Watford /
Hertfordshire WD24 5AD
T +44 (0)1923 818282 / F +44 (0)1923 818280
sales@shopkit.com
www.shopkit.com

Stocks Taylor Benson Ltd
1 Grove Court / Grove Park / Leicester LE19 1SA
T +44 (0)116 240 5600 / F +44 (0)116 240 5601
trevor@stbdesign.co.uk
www.stbdesign.co.uk

Substrakt
Studio 39 / Fazeley Studios / 191 Fazeley Street /
Digbeth / Birmingham B5 5SE
T +44 (0)121 224 7422
team@substrakt.co.uk
www.substrakt.co.uk

TAK!
Studio 204 / The Custard Factory /
Birmingham B9 4AA
T +44 (0)121 288 2528
studio@taktak.net
www.taktak.net

taniemedia
68 Great Eastern Street Ground Floor /
London EC2A 3JT
T +44 (0)20 7739 2762 / F +44 (0)20 8082 5361
contact@taniemedia.com
info@taniemedia.com
www.taniemedia.com

Taxi Studio
93 Princess Victoria Street / Clifton /
Bristol BS8 4DD
T+44 (0)117 973 5151 / F+44 (0)117 973 5181
alex@taxistudio.co.uk
www.taxistudio.co.uk

threebrand
Boat 1502U / The Shore / Leith /
Edinburgh EH6 6QW
T +44 (0)131 454 2030
campbell@threebrand.com
www.threebrand.com

Tijuana
71 Queens Road / Bristol BS8 1QP
T +44 (0)117 910 2440
info@tijuanadesign.com
www.tijuanadesign.com

Turquoise
Suite G First Floor Holborn Hall /
193–197 High Holborn / London WC1V 7BD
T +44 (0)20 7831 2803 / F +44 (0)20 7430 9838
hello@turquoisebranding.com
www.turquoisebranding.com

Two by Two
348 Goswell Road / London EC1V 7LQ
T +44 (0)207 278 1122 / F +44 (0)207 278 1155
zebra@twobytwo.co.uk
www.twobytwo.co.uk

Universal Everything
T +44 (0)7595 512 975
studio@universaleverything.com
www.universaleverything.com

Philip Watts Design
Unit 11: Byron Industrial Estate / Brookfield Road /
Arnold / Nottingham / NG5 7ER
T +44 (0)115 926 9756 / F +44 (0)115 920 5395
sales@philipwattsdesign.com
www.philipwattsdesign.com

Wildwood Creative
Capital Tower / 91 Waterloo Road /
London SE1 8RT
T +44 (0)20 7928 4343 / F +44 (0)20 7928 1144
info@wildwoodcreative.co.uk
www.wildwoodcreative.co.uk

James Williamson Design Ltd
Unit 18 – New Crescent Yard / Acton Lane /
London NW10 8SJ
T +44 (0)208 965 0804
james@jameswilliamson.com
www.jameswilliamson.com

Z3 Design Studio
Studio 2 / Broughton Works / 27 George Street /
Birmingham B3 1QG
T +44 (0)121 233 2545
www.designbyz3.com

PUBLICATION DATA

Publisher
BIS Publishers bv
Het Sieraad Building
Postjesweg 1
1057 DT Amsterdam
The Netherlands
T +31 (0)20 515 02 30
F +31 (0)20 515 02 39
E bis@bispublishers.nl
www.bispublishers.nl

Sales Management
Marijke Wervers
marijke@bispublishers.nl

Production Coordination
Bite grafische vormgeving, Amsterdam
bite@euronet.nl

Design & Art Direction
Taxi Studio, Bristol
www.taxistudio.co.uk

Café Photography
Joakim Borén
www.joakimborén.com

Article
Ben Terrett, London
www.noisydecentgraphics.typepad.com

Preface
Lindsay Camp
www.canichangeyourmind.co.uk

Layout
Bite grafische vormgeving, Amsterdam

Text Revision
Jane Bemont
elegant.english@worldonline.nl